New Perspectives in Supervision

Practical models, tools and resources
for supervisors, mentors and chaplains

Susan Marcuccio

First published by Perspective Supervision 2022
New South Wales, Australia
http://www.perspectivesupervision.com.au
Copyright © 2022 Susan Marcuccio

ISBN Paperback: 978-0-6455174-0-8
ISBN Ebook: 978-0-6455174-1-5

Cover Design, Editing and Layout: Jane Beale

Perspective Supervision

LIVING LIFE WITH GREATER CLARITY

Remarks About the Author

"Of all people to write a book on Professional Supervision that has credibility and who is highly regarded in not just teaching about it… but also being excellent as a practitioner of it… it would be Susan Marcuccio!

Her book: *New Perspectives in Supervision - Practical Models, Tools and Resources for Supervisors, Mentors and Chaplains* should be an essential book for those in training, but also for anyone who is a supervisor that needs some fresh tools or wants to understand why they need to get a supervisor to help them go the long journey.

As a Professional Supervisor, I have done most of my training and PD sessions with Susan and have found her to be practical, engaging and passionate to help people in this space. Susan understands chaplaincy, pastoral care, and supervision because she's lived it!"

Ps Chris Smith, NSW & ACT ACC State Secretary,
Supervisor - AAOS, Recognised Supervisor - Chaplaincy Australia

"I had the delight of first meeting Susan a few years ago when we were co-training a group in professional supervision in Sydney. A passion for the strength of 'good supervision' has slowly seeped into my bones over the years, and I saw immediately that Susan shared this same passion. Since then, we've trained quite a few groups together… a source of joy for me. We've both experienced how professional supervision 'done well' can enrich and bolster a person's professional (and even personal) life, and indeed save a vocational passion and purpose from a downward spiral when the going gets tough.

In many ways, Susan and I approach supervision and teaching from complementary ends of the spectrum, but our passion and purpose is the same. Susan is an insightful, enthusiastic, and creative teacher and supervisor, and I've learnt so much from her over the years. I've often heard students and colleagues alike beg her to write down her many creative and engaging insights (and all her wonderful models, tools, and resources), and I am so delighted she's finally done that!

For a long time, I've seen Susan work tirelessly to promote Professional Supervision, only because she believes wholeheartedly in the transformative process both professionally and personally. She believes that when we engage in transformative reflection with someone who can hold us gently and firmly in that reflective space, that we transform and grow in ways we could not imagine. And she knows that when we do that as practitioners, then those who engage with us in this place are transformed also. I'm honoured to call Susan a colleague and friend, and happily endorse this first of many projects!"

Dinah Eades Buchanan
(M. Couns. Grad Dip Gestalt. Grad Dip Spiritual Direction)
Founder of 'Opening To Grace'
Clinical Supervisor, Psychotherapist, Spiritual Director and Educator

"With over a decade of experience in chaplaincy and supervision (as a chaplain, chaplaincy and supervision trainer, state leader for a chaplaincy organisation, leader in a national supervision association and national leader of a supervision network), coupled with extensive research in the field of supervision, Susan Marcuccio brings a wealth of experience and depth of insight into this fresh new resource.

Susan's ability to transform supervision theory into creative models and tools that facilitate a reflective space for those in pastoral work is nothing short of inspirational. As someone who has experienced the practical empowerment of her presentations, and enrichment in supervision through use of her models and tools, I am excited that her work is finally in print!

It is my hope that this resource will find its way into the hands of many professionals and practitioners, enhancing the work of supervision worldwide."

Ps Leeanne Cameron, DRCN Chaplain,
ACC Pastor - Professional Supervisor

"Working with Susan Marcuccio is like a warm hug on a speed boat! She is both an encouraging presence and a fast-moving visionary, but the adventure is invigorating, and the "scenery" of her insight brings powerful perspectives. I have been inspired in my work alongside Susan as National Director of the Supervision & Mentoring Program of Chaplaincy Australia and also as the Chair of Training Standards on the Board of the Australasian Association of Supervision (AAOS).

Susan is making ground-breaking contributions in the areas of Supervision, Chaplaincy & Mentoring, passionately initiating networks and conversations while strategically developing models, tools and resources. She has a profound impact on those in helping roles, bringing the heart of a Chaplain at a personal level while pioneering across professions to bring significant organisational and cultural change in these sectors.

Her models are practical & grounded in best practice, accessible to both the new and experienced practitioners or helping professionals who are themselves clients of supervision and mentoring. Using her tools and resources in my own pastoral supervision practice has led to rich experiences of reflection and transformation. Her innovative ideas are easy to implement and adapt to various supervision, chaplaincy, and mentoring contexts, both clinical and pastoral.

I wholeheartedly recommend: *New Perspectives in Supervision: Practical Models, Tools and Resources for Supervisors, Mentors and Chaplains* to refresh and enlarge your professional experience."

Alison Martin, Recognised Professional Supervisor,
National Supervision & Mentoring Coordinator, Chaplaincy Australia
Grad. Cert. Professional Supervision (Clinical/Pastoral),
B. Social Work, Cert IV Christian Counselling & Family Therapy

"If compassion is the superpower of those who would offer Pastoral Care, then Supervision is an indispensable aspect of the framework that ensures that we do it well and are able to keep doing it! Susan is uniquely positioned to provide inspiration and direction to all those who would provide Supervision, Mentoring and Pastoral Care.

Over the last ten years I have had the privilege of working alongside Susan as she has explored, developed and tested useful models for enhancing the effectiveness and longevity of those who would provide pastoral care and support to others.

I have seen her work as a pastor, chaplain, supervisor, mentor and entrepreneur. She is a great leader and a trusted friend who is passionate about seeing others well supported, urging them forward as they seek to fulfil their passions and goals.

Her understanding and insights in the areas of supervision and mentoring provide fresh and effective tools for each of us to use. When she speaks about these subjects, people stop to listen. I hope that you will join them and allow yourself the opportunity to gain some *New Perspectives*."

Ralph Estherby, National Director Chaplaincy Australia,
Pastor & Military Chaplain

"In 2021, I completed a 'Graduate Certificate in Professional Supervision' through St. Mark's in Canberra. I was blessed to have Susan Marcuccio as one of the trainers. I started the course with some anxiety and was unsure about being a supervisor.

Under Susan's gentle guidance, encouragement and wisdom, I was transformed. Supervision changed from being something that had to be done, to something that was both life-giving and enjoyable. It has now become my part-time ministry!

In 2022 I have joined Susan for several profound Professional Development sessions, as well as 'Creative Group Supervision.' Susan has the rare ability to make theory come alive through practice. Her models of supervision are easy to understand and easy to apply.

Susan has an abundance of practical resources that release supervision from being merely word-based. All of this has come from her vast ministry and supervision experience. I can't wait to read about her journey and delve into her long-anticipated book. It is truly a gift to supervisors and supervisees alike."

Rev. Frank Van Der Korput, BA, B.Th.,
MA (Chaplaincy). Dip (Dementia), GCPS.

"Susan Marcuccio's expertise and professional approach to supervision is inspiring. She has a gentle and considered way of crafting a supervision session, which can be modified according to the needs presented. The approach to supervision and mentoring is empowering for supervisees and mentees.

I have experienced Susan's professional and structured models in group supervision with her and have noted the ease with which she facilitates a group session.

She provides training to others to be effective in the provision of meaningful supervision and has developed helpful models and tools to assist in this process. I highly recommend her book: *New Perspectives in Supervision: Practical Models, Tools and Resources for Supervisors, Mentors and Chaplains.*"

Dr Amanda Nickson, Social Worker, Pastor, Supervisor,
Author and Speaker at Interactive Solutions

Dedication & Acknowledgements

I would like to dedicate this book to my amazing sister Jane, who inspired me and assisted me so much in the writing of this book. I literally could not have done it without you. So, Jane, thank you, thank you, thank you for the many hours you have worked on this project, for always believing in me, and for helping me to make this dream a reality!

To my wonderful husband Stephen, to my kids and grandkids, and all my family, you are everything to me and I want to thank you all for championing me on always.

To my faithful friends and colleagues who always encourage me, are there for me with a coffee and a listening ear. I am so thankful and grateful for each one of you.

I would like to also acknowledge the incredible supervisors, mentors, coaches and teachers I have had over the years; I have learnt so much from each one of you and am truly thankful for your investment in me. To have a safe place to go for support and to learn and grow has literally been life changing for me.

For those I have had the privilege to supervise and mentor, I never take it for granted that I get to do what I love, and I am truly thankful that you trust me enough to let me walk alongside you for part of your journey.

For those who have shared their stories with me in my role as a chaplain, I have been profoundly impacted by your courage, resilience and the trust you showed in me, allowing me to sit with you in sometimes your darkest hour.

To all those who are now reading *New Perspectives in Supervision*, I thank you for taking the time to pick up this book and to hear some of my story. My hope for you is that you are impacted in a way that will make you think about your *own* passion, purpose and calling and that you too will begin to see new perspectives!

And finally, I would like to thank my Lord and Saviour Jesus Christ, who has transformed my life and given me love, hope and joy beyond anything I could ever have imagined!

CONTENTS

Disclaimer

Some names, and other identifiers have been omitted or changed, for confidentiality reasons. In telling my story, I am cognisant that I am writing about events that happened from my perspective and memories. I do not presume to recount the life events, memories or experiences of others who appear in this book.

Preface

When we see the world through the lens of new perspectives, we see things differently. We develop an ability to reflect on situations and gain a greater understanding of ourselves. Importantly we begin to see and reflect on what might be happening for others.

How does a life change when a person has new perspectives? For myself and the people I have had the privilege to walk alongside, the most amazing transformations have taken place. I am so in awe of the positive changes I have witnessed, that I am just so excited to share some of them with you.

Experience has shown me that with new perspectives, we:

- live life with greater clarity
- find our purpose
- connect to our unique calling
- flourish and grow as an individual
- develop a new appreciation for the experiences of those around us

For many years I tried to find my purpose. I put time and energy into 'things' that I was passionate about. I longed for that feeling that told me I had found the 'right' thing to do with my life. I willingly changed paths and explored multiple options, but nothing seemed to hit the mark.

During this period, I remember feeling grateful and blessed, but I also felt frustrated. Outwardly I did my best with whatever was before me. Inwardly, my inner voice pleaded with me to keep looking:

"There must be more!" I would tell myself. "I mustn't settle - not yet!"

Then one day I found it! What a day that was!!

Everything changed for me - my focus, my job satisfaction and...

My perspective!

Introduction

When I decided it was time to officially register my supervision business, I found myself wrestling with different names. Then almost out of nowhere, the word *perspective* appeared before me. That was it!

Perspective Supervision - Living Life with Greater Clarity

New Perspectives in Supervision has been developed over many years as I have continually discovered *new* ways of seeing the world through the lens of *new* perspectives. I've known for a long time that I needed to write a book about these *new* perspectives – about the clarity they have provided for myself and those I've worked with. By documenting my stories and providing my models, tools and resources, I'm fulfilling an important purpose in my life:

To give others the opportunity to discover
their *own* new perspectives!

New Perspectives in Supervision has been written for supervisors and mentors as well as those who provide chaplaincy or pastoral care. If you are learning to be a supervisor or chaplain, or you are a student or professional in a related field, then this book is also for you.

Whatever your background, if you are wanting greater insight into how to care for yourself or others in different situations, you might also find this book helpful.

I've also aimed the content at people who themselves *engage* in supervision or mentoring. In fact, having the opportunity to be the *supervisee* is a process that I find to be life changing. When I am the person on the receiving end, I get the chance to experience the benefits of supervision firsthand. Having someone really see me, really listen to me and not judge me allows me to feel safe enough to be myself. As this happens, I find myself coming out from behind a wall – sometimes a wall that I didn't realise I'd constructed in an effort to feel safe.

Having supervision enables me to be my authentic self. But at first, it took some getting used to! It actually felt quite indulgent when another person created a confidential space that was *all about me!* I realised though, over time, that it's not just a 'helpful' or 'nice' thing to do - supervision is ESSENTIAL if I'm going to reach my potential. Supervision is fundamental to me being all I was created to be and to doing all that I was created to do.

Supervision has assisted me to see how all of the following things impact on what I do:

⇨ my beliefs
⇨ my passion
⇨ my purpose
⇨ what I value in life
⇨ how I make meaning out of experiences
⇨ the way I see the world

Join me as I write about connecting with people who felt alone. Learn with me as I discovered how to walk *alongside* others for part of their journey. There are heart-warming stories of breakthrough, including recounts of people feeling 'heard' and 'seen' – sometimes for the first time in their lives. These encounters will hopefully stir you to consider new perspectives in listening, being fully present, and gaining real insight into situations that you haven't come across before.

I've divided the book into chapters, with sections on models, tools and resources. As we travel together through the pages, I will reveal to you how the practice of supervision assisted me through difficult and challenging times and led to me developing my first supervision model – the three ringed model.

New Perspectives in Supervision is suitable to read from cover to cover or may be used as a reference tool, with individual topics chosen according to your purpose or learning objective.

If you are currently researching the similarities and subtle differences between the modalities of supervision, mentoring and chaplaincy, you will have the chance to learn more about each of these roles. As I guide you to view the stories and resources through the different lenses of each domain, you might find you begin to identify with having a calling for one or more roles.

As you read through this book, my hope is that your eyes will open to see things differently – with new perspectives. As you are stirred to connect to your own unique calling, you will be taking important steps to engage in transformational learning and to living your life with greater clarity.

It made such a difference to my life when I had the courage to do what I *knew* I was called to do. Let me tell you something important – it was *not* what others wanted me to do.

So, this book is for anyone who wants to step into the 'very thing' that they are made to do and to be the person that they were *made to be*. Regardless of your beliefs, we are all human and all want our lives to mean something. We all want to be able to live a meaningful life.

Coming to this realisation for the first time was spectacularly enlightening! It was like someone turned a light on and I could now see what previously was in darkness!

So, as you hold this book in your hand right now, my message to you is:

"Don't spend your life stumbling around in the dark - turn the light on! You will be amazed at what you will start to see!"

Finally, New Perspectives in Supervision is designed to further equip you to come alongside others. As you do, you will be in a position to help them to flourish. Armed with models, tools and resources, you will be ready to assist others to be seen and heard, and to connect with what gives them life and hope.

May you truly live your life to the full and encounter many new perspectives in supervision and beyond.

Chapters Overview

This book can be read by choosing individual chapters or by looking up individual models, tools and resources, however, it has been written in a way that builds chapter by chapter.

Below is a summary of the chapters in order, to give you an overview of the book and how it progresses.

This 'Chapters Overview' outlines why I have included each of these topics and will hopefully give you a sense of what you will gain by reading the chapters in this order:

Chapter One is really all about you. Considering your purpose, your calling, your passion, what's important to you and what gives your life meaning.

I have shared some of my story in this chapter to help you know me and to see how I connected with my calling. I think it really gives a good foundation to this book. It will help you understand my motivation and why certain things are important to me.

I hope it will also encourage you once you read my story that there is hope for everyone. While many of the things I have experienced over my life have been incredibly difficult and painful, my hope is that by sharing some of my story, it will inspire you to be all that you can be and to find your own unique calling and purpose.

Chapter Two is all about honouring a person's story, to be reminded how important it is to listen, really listen, to be present in the moment with people and to show empathy. Everyone has a story, and some people get to share theirs. If you get this privilege, to hear someone's story, then lean in and let them know that their story matters. Sharing your story with someone can make it less heavy - how wonderful it is to have someone really hear you and genuinely care.

This chapter shares some of the encounters I had over time that really impacted me and taught me so much. I have learnt that nothing is wasted and everything that I have experienced has made me who I am today. I'm still becoming all I want to be but I'm learning to accept who I am and that I'm doing all I can to live a life that honours others and shows kindness and care to those I have the privilege to meet.

This chapter is an important foundation for the book as it shows how important each person and their unique story is.

Chapter Three is where I introduce the concept of supervision. For some people reading this book, supervision is your profession and I hope that this chapter will assist you by having a model you can use to explain supervision to others, and as a tool to use for goal setting and reflection. For other readers, you may have no idea what I mean by supervision.

I'm hopeful that by the end of this chapter you will have much more clarity about what the profession of supervision is and how it differs to other helping professions. I also include a section on the heart of chaplaincy and the need for mentors. I have called this chapter 'Unwrapping the Gift of Supervision', as that is how I see it. As you start to unwrap it for yourself and the various layers are revealed, I hope that you see why it is such a gift for each person that engages with it.

Chapter Four considers the concept of story and process. In this chapter, we are reminded of the importance of a person's story but look at how some people might get stuck right in the middle of their story, to the point that they *can't see out*. This is where new perspectives come in.

When we are looking at our story from within it, we can only see things from one aspect. When we step out of our story for a moment, we can see it very differently. We can see new perspectives. We gain clarity about our situation. While having someone sit with us in our pain is what's needed at some points in our life, having someone help us to step out of our story for a moment is what's needed at other times.

In this chapter, I introduce two models to help people step out of their story and into a process to help them gain clarity and see things from a broader perspective.

Chapter Five is a reminder that situations come into our lives that challenge us and change us. At times, these situations have the potential to take us out of the race or leave us just existing rather than living life to the full.

In this chapter I share some of my own personal experience with loss and grief, including what I experienced and learnt. I give some of the insights that have helped me to have resilience and *go the distance* while keeping connected to my calling.

I'm hopeful that this chapter will encourage you to do whatever you need to do to build internal fortitude so that circumstances can't stop you and you can go on to live the life you have always dreamed of - one that is meaningful and full of purpose. Also, to know that it's this very thing, your unique calling, that can keep you going when you feel like your world has shattered and you can't go on. In other words, how to not just bounce back, but to *bounce forward*.

Chapter Six is about caring and being cared for. In this chapter, I talk about what a privilege it is to walk alongside people as they journey through life. Also, the importance of being careful to not just 'go through the process' without ensuring that you have made a connection with the person.

I talk about the dangers of becoming *too mechanical* when we try to follow formulas or try to get someone into the process of supervision - we may be getting it technically correct but miss the importance of the relationship and the connection we make.

To 'have awareness,' to 'consider our response' and to 'always look to empower' are all elements of the model that I have developed to ensure that we remember to care. Being cared for ourselves is also part of this chapter. I look at self-care issues and strategies as well as introducing a model designed to enhance your work and life.

Chapter Seven looks at the important topic of worldview, vision and values. In this chapter, we explore how a person's worldview really impacts the way they see and experience the world around them. Being mindful of this really changes how we interact with people. It reminds us to stop and consider what might be happening for them - to realise there is often much more going on for people than we initially see. Also, to avoid assuming *we know* when we really don't due to not even considering the situation from their perspective.

Another area covered in this chapter is around vision and values and how they impact what we do. There is an activity to assist with identifying whether someone is vision driven, values driven or both. This chapter finishes with the importance of continual personal and professional development.

Chapter Eight has a focus on emotions and boundaries. We take 'building connection with someone' to a whole new level. We start off getting awareness of how we are feeling at any given time and the impact our feelings have on those around us.

We practise using a model that *slows down* the whole process of an interaction with someone and assists us to consider what's happening for them and for us. Through the model, we find a whole new perspective on the situation and interaction that we have with someone.

We also look in this chapter at boundaries, advanced empathy, triggers, transference, reflecting feelings and validation. We take a peek into the box of emotions and consider how to manage our lives using boundaried spaces.

Chapter Nine looks at the important topic of reflective practice. In this chapter, we look at what reflective practice is and how it is such a foundational aspect of supervision.

Many of the creative tools are found in this chapter, with information about how and why I created them, and how they play a major part in assisting people to gain new perspectives. To have something concrete to focus on assists people to step out of their story and their abstract thoughts for a moment to gain that broader picture and to see things differently.

The tools here include: drawing your scenario, having a voice and theological reflection.

There is also a section where I encourage and empower you to come up with your own creative tools to assist people to engage in reflective practice.

Chapter Ten is about working with groups of people rather than just individuals. While the focus is on group supervision, the ideas presented in this chapter can be used with many different types of groups.

There's also a section on *creative group supervision* in which I highlight how to use creative tools not just with individuals but in groups, both face to face and online.

This chapter covers preparing for group supervision and provides information on group guidelines. I outline step by step how to run a group and use creative tools.

CHAPTER ONE

FINDING YOUR PURPOSE, PASSION & CALLING

Connect to your calling
Pursue your purpose
Know your meaning
Do what excites you
Live your life
Do it today!

Get up
Start dreaming
Don't give up
Learn from your mistakes
Don't be afraid to fail
Give it everything you have!

Be courageous
Be bold
Be free from others' expectations
Live authentically
Live your life to the full
You can do it!

How I Became Connected to My Calling

I had never felt more judged or alone as I walked down the main street of my local town. I'd just been given the news that I was pregnant. Being only 16 years old brought with it glances of disapproval from those I had told, and I felt the guilt of letting everybody down.

When I heard the news from the doctor that I was pregnant, I was at a point in my life where I didn't really care what happened to me, so I took stupid risks and made bad choices. The moment I heard the news that I was pregnant, I realised I had someone else to consider, and I believe that literally saved my life. I was offered an abortion by the doctor as an option, but I never even considered it, so I guess we saved each other's life…

I had recently dropped out of school at age 15. It was the end of Year 10 and I was terrified of sitting the exam that needed to be passed to progress to Year 11. It was easier to drop out than admit to everyone that I was scared to fail.

I had a part time retail job and managed to get fulltime work, so it was easy to leave. School for me was a social event where I did just enough to get by. I loved maths and social science and in my earlier school years got good marks but by Year 10, I just stopped trying and didn't really care about my future.

This was at a time in my life when I had recently moved out of home. I went to stay with a friend who just happened to live with a group of other people, and I just never went back home. So, I sort of slid out rather than announcing I was leaving. My boyfriend lived at the house I was staying at which was the main reason I went to stay there.

After I became pregnant, and the house was raided by police, my boyfriend and I left and got a flat together.

The judgement I felt sitting in the police station as a pregnant teenager was horrible. The police quickly realised I was not involved in the illegal activity but were quick to tell me my life was going nowhere. The good news part of this story is I gave birth to a beautiful baby girl who has been one of the delights of my life. I was then on a mission to give her the best life I could.

I came to Australia from England on a boat with my parents when I was 4 years old and moved to Kangaroo Island. It was an idyllic location to grow up, alongside my younger brother and sister. We had a wonderful childhood, with farm animals, beautiful beaches and all the adventures you can have living on an island. We moved to the big city when I was 12 which was a huge culture shock. That's when my slide into destructive behaviour began.

Feeling alone and not good enough, I stopped trying to better myself and just indulged in partying and getting into lots of trouble with my new city friends. I used to come home from school and ride my father's motorbike around the garden. I decided I wanted to be a motorbike stunt rider, so spent many hours practicing. I was happy to take risks as I didn't really care what happened to me. I also went trailbike riding with friends which I loved.

After three years living in the city, we moved as a family back to another state to a quieter location. I found the change really hard as I had left a large group of friends in the city who had basically been my life. I found myself feeling very alone at first but soon made some friends at my new school and started getting in trouble again.

After only 6 months, I had reached the end of Year 10 and was dropping out of school. My final day of school had a fitting end - my father asked me where my end of year report was and I answered: "I think it's in the bin at school…"

Eventually my boyfriend and I married when I was 18 years old. I had lived for a while at my parent's place in a caravan as a single mother before we got married. I felt like such a failure so went back to him and we got married. Almost a year later, we had a precious baby boy. I had decided to have another child so our daughter would have a sibling. After living in council houses and rental properties for a few years, we finally bought our first home.

When I was 21, after a near car accident where I thought for a moment that I was going to die, I had the profound experience of wondering what would have happened to me if I had died. It started me on a quest to find out. Eventually, I asked my sister if I could go with her to her church, as I thought maybe they would have the answer.

The moment I walked into the church and heard the music playing, I thought to myself:

"This is fantastic, why didn't someone tell me about this before?"

At the end of the service, the preacher asked if anyone wanted to come out the front, say a prayer and give their life to God. I was straight out there:

"Of course, I do!!"

My life was never the same after that moment. It's hard to explain but I was filled with the most amazing love and hope and felt like a brand-new person. As I learnt about Jesus, how he was filled with compassion, and fought for justice and cared for people, especially those no one else wanted, I just knew that I wanted to spend the rest of my life becoming more like him.

From that day it was like my eyes were opened and I could see people in need everywhere I went. It was almost overwhelming. I desperately wanted people to know that someone cared about them - that there was hope. I just knew that God had called me to care for others, to get the message out to people:

"You are not alone."

I started to notice things that were happening in the world. I remember watching images of children starving in Africa and thinking - people are dying!!! Why is no one doing anything??

I realised quite quickly that I couldn't save the whole world so I decided to study the Bible to learn more about this incredible Jesus. I learnt that he was moved with compassion to action, that he cared about *the many* and *the one and* that we were to speak up for those who didn't have a voice - to show mercy, kindness, love and grace to people rather than show partiality and judgement. That was someone I could dedicate my life to.

A couple of years later, I had the opportunity to travel to Europe and Morocco with my father and sister and my two kids. It was such an amazing experience; the kids went to an Arabic speaking school and we immersed ourselves in the culture. Being a fairly new Christian in a Muslim country only strengthened my faith but also helped me to listen to and respect others that had a different belief.

I was keen to learn and to understand what it was like for someone to live in a culture that told you what you *had to believe* and could enforce it *by law*. Those who lived there and became a Christian were often shunned by their family and possibly arrested. The stakes were high, and it made me really value the freedom we have in Australia.

By the time I was around 25 years old, I was again living as a single mother and had started my own business to support myself. I had a business making and selling clothes. I had two different shops and also sold items from home. I learnt a lot about running a small successful business but one day after being up half the night making orders, I decided I'd had enough and just stopped. I had hoped to make enough money to fund overseas missions to help those in need, but it was just too much work for too little money.

After that I had various sales jobs and also started volunteering in the church office. It was there that I learnt to do administration work. Then I started running computer courses for other volunteers in the church office. I would learn how to do something myself and then teach it to others the next day.

Over time, I started serving in a number of leadership positions in the church which I really loved. It was so great to be part of something bigger than myself and being able to help others and to share the hope that I myself had found. It was around this time that I considered studying social work as I desperately wanted a career that would help people. But I was given advise against it, so I didn't end up pursuing this line of work. I remember at the time being so disappointed. I was also going to apply to be a flight attendant as I loved traveling but as a single mum, it wasn't really an option for me.

Just before my 31st birthday I remarried, this time to someone who shared my faith. We had six children between us but tragically my husband's 18-year-old son died in a car accident just before we got together. I will never forget the moment I heard about the accident. I was standing at the back of the church. Everyone was stunned. People kept turning up at the church as they heard the news. I was so moved with compassion and remember desperately wanting to be a support to those that were suffering so much. It was one of the defining moments of my life that was leading me to my calling.

Not long after we got married, we moved interstate with four of our children and attended a church where we both ended up working fulltime as Pastors. My focus was on overseas missions, especially to Africa, but the church also had projects in Russia and Indonesia. I oversaw local missions which included setting up a counselling centre, sourcing government funding, setting up a rehab for women with addictions and running a variety of programs and services in the church and local community. I loved working in these areas, but I still felt that there was something more and that I still hadn't really found my dream profession.

I had heard about chaplaincy and it sounded like it could be a good fit for me, so I decided to go to the local hospital and do a short introductory chaplaincy training course. The first day I was sitting in the class listening to the trainer, I almost leapt in my chair – someone else felt the same as I did about caring for people!!!! I was so excited, I felt like I had finally found *my thing*.

The trainer talked about having compassion, empathy, listening, really listening to people, showing respect and not being judgemental. It was everything I had been looking for. I said to myself, that day:

"One day, I will be training a chaplaincy course just like this."

I completed the short course, but circumstances prevented me from pursuing it any further at that point - I was devastated.

A few years later, I was looking out the window of the church where I was working and I had another defining moment. I suddenly realised that there were people everywhere out there that thought nobody cared about them - people who were *alone and suffering*. I just knew I had to get out of the church building and back into the community - so I quit my job as a pastor, stayed at the church as a volunteer and studied to be a chaplain.

I worked at a local picture theatre doing marketing to fund my chaplaincy training. One day while I was at work at the theatre, I received a phone call telling me that I had got the job that I had applied for as a fulltime hospital chaplain. I was beyond excited. I had completed my chaplaincy training and had started to look for chaplaincy jobs. I had felt confident at this interview and was just so delighted to be successful. It was everything I hoped it would be - I loved every minute!

After about 12 months working in the role as a hospital chaplain, I was offered a job as a fulltime chaplaincy trainer. I remembered the vision I'd had that first day when I sat in the chaplaincy course about one day being able to train a chaplaincy course. I was so thankful to be presented with the opportunity to train others, so I accepted the position.

I still did some chaplaincy work in hospitals and as a disaster responder as I didn't want to give up the role that I loved altogether. I travelled all over Australia teaching chaplaincy for many years. It was such a privilege and I learnt so much about being a chaplain and how to care for people from the practical experiences but also by researching, writing, teaching and learning from others.

My team and I ended up training literally thousands of chaplains. Due to the success of the training, I was offered a job overseeing all the vocational training courses in the college I was working for. It was a chance to grow and learn so I accepted the role and worked doing this for a number of years.

My first week at the college, I was having lunch with several of the staff and they were all talking about the books they had written. I felt so intimidated but also inspired and thought that I would love to write a book one day - and here I am, writing my first book!

Being in such an incredible culture of learning, I decided to embark on my own studies and it was a very proud day when *the girl who had dropped out of high school* graduated with a Master of Arts degree.

While I was working at the college, I was offered a chaplaincy leadership role so did this part time as well. Although I did like the leadership roles, I realised I had moved away from the core of what I really felt called to – *caring for others.*

When I became a chaplain, I was told it was mandatory to have supervision. I didn't even know what supervision was. I was a very private person, used to dealing with things by myself and protecting myself from being judged by others. So, when my supervisor asked me in my first session how I felt, my response was:

"How do you want me to feel?"

Eventually over time I started to trust my supervisor and realised it was a safe place to share how I really felt.

It was life changing!

My whole life, I had learnt to just rely on myself, to have a tough exterior, to be able to just hang on and get by and I had done it well. But with supervision, I found out that there was another way...

How amazing it was to have someone sit with me and really listen to me without an agenda. They weren't trying to get me to do something for them - they just genuinely cared, had appropriate boundaries and were allowing me to express what *I wanted* to.

It was so great to feel heard. Eventually, I felt brave and safe enough to honestly share my feelings and to use the space to grow, heal and learn new things about myself. How grateful I am that it was mandatory, as I doubt I would have pursued it myself and I would have missed out on so much.

I was so impacted by my own experience of supervision that I decided to train to be a supervisor. The day I graduated from the supervision course and became a recognised supervisor was one of the happiest days of my life. I realised that as a chaplain, I could make a difference for *the one*, which is important. But by becoming a supervisor, I could make a difference for *the many*, due to the multiplication effect.

I realised that if I could support those who cared for others, and they thrived and stayed in their roles, then many more people would be supported and cared for. If I could support those who lead churches or organisations - if those leaders were healthy and thriving, then their teams would be healthy and thriving and those who sought to join their churches or organisations would have great experiences and be well looked after.

As I thought it through, I realised the potential impact and how much I loved this multiplication effect!

I decided to become an advocate for supervision with a passion to:

> *See all those in the helping professions receive*
> *quality, non-judgmental, confidential support*
> *and engage in transformational learning*

Today, I have a vision for a Supervision and Mentoring Program that will enable accessibility and facilitate high quality supervision and mentoring. I run my own private practice called Perspective Supervision, named so as I believe that *perspective* is such a key part of supervision:

> *Perspective Supervision - Living life with greater clarity!*

Having experienced searching for many years to find my own unique calling, I am passionate about the journeys of others as they each move towards finding their own unique purpose and calling.

How You Can Connect to Your Calling

In order to assist people to find and connect to their own unique calling, I developed a simple tool that I use in supervision. It can however be used by anyone who wants to find their purpose and be really clear about their passion, including what is most important to them.

I also use this tool when I am running professional development workshops as it is quick and easy to use. You may like to try this for yourself and then try it with others.

CONNECTING TO YOUR CALLING TOOL

Step 1: Finish the following statements

⇨ I feel passionate about…

⇨ I feel energised when…

⇨ I love it when I get to…

⇨ I would love to be a voice for…

⇨ What's most important for me is…

⇨ The thing that drives me is…

⇨ Anything else you would like to add…

Step 2: Read out what you have written and see what you notice

This is where you can look for themes, see what you notice about what you have written, and see how you feel about it. Hopefully if you have really connected with your calling through this activity and you have written about what is really important to you, you will feel a bit emotional and motivated.

Step 3: Circle all the main words that stand out to you

As you read through all of your sentences, you will most likely notice that some words really stand out. There may even be words that you have repeated a number of times. Circle these key words so you end up with a list.

You can sometimes group the words as well if there are some that seem to go together.

Step 4: Number the key words in order of importance to you

Go through the list and choose which of the key words represents what is most important to you, with ONE being of highest value.

Step 5: The start of discovering your values

The list you have developed can be used as the start of discovering your core values, that is, the things that are really important to you and non-negotiable in your life. This can be really helpful in your quest to live a life that has purpose and meaning.

Step 6: Connect to your calling

Using the statements you made at the start, and the key words that you have now discovered, you can begin to get a sense of 'what it is' that you are 'called to do' and 'called to be'.

Are there ways that you can start to move towards living a life that is congruent with what you have now discovered?

It's never too late to get started. What can you do today? Don't settle for less than living life to the full!

Living Life to the Full

What does it mean to really live life to the full? I thought I knew until one day when I had a significant moment with a grumpy elderly gentleman. This man ended up teaching me so much.

After weeks of going to this particular gentleman's room in my role as a hospital chaplain and offering him chaplaincy visits, he finally invited me in to talk. He had just been moved into a private room from a six-bed ward. After taking a while to tell me some of his story, he pointed to the window and referred to his view of 'just a concrete carpark'.

I will never forget what happened next - he suddenly stopped talking and looked straight at me. Here was a man, a very grumpy man, stuck in a room with only a concrete carpark to look at, no green grass or really anything living. In the final days of his life and in this particular moment, he decided he had to give me a message. It was a real wake up call. He said these words to me:

"Make sure you live life to the full."

It really hit me and I pondered on what he said that evening.

The next day, I went into his room to see him - and he wasn't there. His slippers were still next to his bed. I went to try and find someone who could tell me where he was and found out he'd died over night. I was so impacted. The slippers were so symbolic, still next to his bed, but would never be worn by him again.

On what ended up being the last day of his life, he had given me the message:

"Live life to the full."

At first, I thought he meant *cram as much into life as you can*. As I reflected on the meaning of his message over the next few days, I found myself walking to my car from the train station. I noticed for the first time the bright red bottle brushes. I was captivated by the colour and the fact that I had never noticed them before. In that moment, I realised he meant to *really live each day* - to see the beauty in *every moment*.

WOW! That moment with him forever changed me...

Connected to Your Calling and Staying in Your Lane

When I was asked to choose a ward in the hospital for my chaplaincy training placement, I knew straight away that I wanted the Emergency Ward. This is where there were people suffering alone. People who started their day just like everyone else, unaware that the unthinkable would happen and they would end up in an emergency ward.

My first day in the ward I was so excited. I quickly learnt the importance of staying in my role and being a supportive part of the team. I met so many incredibly brave people in the Emergency Ward.

An experience that has stayed with me is when I was asked to go to a particular room to assist a family. I walked to the entrance of the room and saw a lady in the bed with three young girls in school uniforms lying all over her. In the corner was her husband and her mother. I was invited in, and her husband told me that his wife had cancer and had taken a turn for the worst; it looked like the end was imminent.

He asked me to stay in the room with them for a while as it gave them comfort. For the next hour or so I stayed with them. What a privilege to be invited into this sacred space with them. I remember feeling so sad that these girls were about to lose their mother. It felt like I was doing nothing, but I came to realise over time how much of a difference *my presence, just being there*, could make for someone, or in this case for an entire family.

I have found that a person's calling can change and expand over time. While my first realisation of my calling was when I found chaplaincy, something I still feel a calling to, my next step was to expand into supervision.

I do occasionally still work in a chaplaincy role, as a hospital locum or disaster response chaplain. And, I am still drawn to people who are suffering alone.

I realised though that it's not just people in disaster zones or emergency wards that are suffering alone; there are people who care for others, including those in leadership positions, who often find themselves with nowhere to go to share about their struggles. These people are often so busy helping others that they have a tendency to neglect looking after themselves.

Experience has shown me that the higher you get in a leadership position, the fewer people you have around you who you can really be vulnerable with. The result of this situation is a difficulty in getting the support you desperately need.

To be able to learn about yourself, you must be able to be brave enough to share and trust someone to *hold the space for you*. I just love that supervision and mentoring provide this space for leaders and any other people who care for others.

It is such a privilege to do the work I do; my sense of fulfillment serves as a constant reminder - *find your lane and stay in it*. I get so energised from doing supervision and mentoring, I just love it, how amazing that I get to do this!

STAYING IN YOUR LANE TOOL

Once you have connected to your calling and discovered your purpose and passion it can be a real challenge to not get side-tracked and end up doing things that are not part of your calling. One way to get real clarity is to use the metaphor of 'staying in your lane.'

Imagine a five-lane highway and you are traveling along the middle lane, your lane. Opportunities in the other lanes can constantly try and lure you into a different lane.

I use this as a tool with people in supervision. You may like to have a go at this yourself and then use it with others to assist them.

Step 1: Draw a five-lane highway

On a piece of paper, draw five lanes like a highway. The middle lane is your lane, where you are living in your passion and purpose, doing what is consistent with your values. The middle lane contains what is important to you - it's where you are connected to your calling.

Ideally, we all just live in this middle lane. Often though, this is not what happens, so it can be helpful to map out what you are doing and get a clear picture of your life. To do that, move onto step 2.

Step 2: Add your roles and responsibilities to the highway

Now get ready to write down everything you do and map it onto the highway. Those things that you know are at the centre of your calling, add to the middle lane. Those things that are close but not quite in the middle lane, add to the ones next to the middle. Those things that are further from your calling, add to the outer lanes.

Step 3: Review the items on your highway

Now take some time to review and reflect on what you have included and the position of the roles and responsibilities on your highway. This will give you a good snapshot of where you currently are in regards to being connected and living in your calling.

Check and see how many things are in the middle lane and how many others are in the other lanes. See what you notice. Mapping it out like this helps you to gain new perspectives.

Step 4: Making changes to stay in your lane

If you notice that all you are doing is in the middle lane, then great. You may need to check just how much is in that lane though as you can try and cram too many things into the middle lane and it can cause a metaphorical car crash. You may need to prioritise your time or the timing of when to engage in what.

If you have lots of things that are not in the middle lane, it may be time to review these things and see if you need to make some changes. If you spread yourself too thin, then you will not be as focused, and you can end up burning out. This is especially true if much of your time is spent doing things that you don't love to do and are not part of your passion, purpose and calling.

Looking at the five lanes becomes a great visual aid to making decisions about what to say no to and what to say yes to in the future. While we can all struggle at times to identify and walk in our calling, it's worth the time and effort to discover our middle lane priorities. When you realise that you have found what belongs there, your life will never be the same again!

Don't settle for less than living in the middle lane - how sad to waste our lives not living out our true potential and our unique purpose and calling. Be who you were made to be and do what you were made to do. Start today!

⬥ ⬥ ⬥

CHAPTER TWO

SUPPORT BEFORE ACTION

Listen, just listen
Don't try and fix me
Stay with me
Tell me you will try
Don't offer me your sympathy
Try and understand

I already feel judged by others
Show me mercy
Show me kindness
It doesn't take much
Just a caring look
Be with me

It's all I need
To not be alone
Try and have empathy
Something to ground me
I will be ok
But first I need you to listen

Presence

I will never forget the day my good friend and colleague pulled me aside and said to me:

"Do you realise how you just came across with that group of people?"

I looked at her and said, "What do you mean?"

She went on to tell me that I came across quite harsh and in task mode and was not really listening to anyone or present in the moment. Feeling horrified and defensive, I reflected on the time I had just spent with my team. In that moment, the realisation hit me. She was right, but I had been totally unaware at the time.

I wasn't sure how to respond but I thanked her for telling me. I then went on to ponder and after a while, I realised what an incredible gift she had just given me. It changed the way that I interacted with people from that day on. I get emotional just thinking about it. What if she hadn't told me?

It's amazing how unaware we can be and just shows the need to have great people around us that will tell us the truth. Communication is so much more that what you say, it's also how people feel when you are around. What you *don't say* often speaks the loudest.

This friend of mine has the most amazing ability to be fully present in the moment with people. I wonder what encounters she had in her life that helped her to see the value in really listening to someone and to be present with them.

It reminds me of another situation that really taught me about the value of just being there and really being present with a person. I was just about to leave the hospital where I was working as a chaplain when I suddenly felt compelled to turn around and go back in. As I did, a nurse came toward me and said:

"I'm so glad you are still here."

She told me that a man had died in one of the wards. She asked me to wait in the visitor's room as the family were with their loved one saying their goodbyes and then were going to make their way into the visitor's room. I sat and waited and then the family slowly walked in.

I was drawn immediately to this frail old lady that made her way to the table with the rest of the family. We made eye contact and I whispered to her:

"Do you want me to come over and sit with you?"

She nodded. I went over and sat next to her, and she took my hand. She then turned to her family who were all sitting at the table having a family discussion about the death of this lovely lady's husband of over 60 years. I sat there with her for about 30 minutes, not saying anything but holding her hand.

She held on tight.

I remember my internal dialogue:

"Should I say something? Should I join the discussion with the family? Should I do something?"

As I looked at this precious lady who had just lost her husband, I somehow listened to her and heard what she *wasn't saying*. This was taking listening and being present to a whole new level. Everything in me wanted to fix the situation for her, to say something profound, to do something but somehow, I kept silent and still and present.

When it was time for them to leave the hospital, she stood up and followed her family to the door of the hospital. As we walked together down the corridors of the hospital to the exit, she continued to hold my hand tightly.

When we got to the exit she let go of my hand and turned and looked me in the eyes and whispered:

"Thank you."

She then turned and was ushered into the waiting car by her family. And then, she was gone.

To this day, it is one of the most humbling, moving experiences of my life. It still evokes emotion in me as I remember that day.

Once she had gone, I left and wept. I cried for her, and for the incredible gift she had just given me. To realise that there was nothing I could say that would make any difference in this situation. I couldn't fix it; I couldn't make it better but what I was invited to do was to 'be with her'.

That is what she needed in that moment - to be connected to another human being. I'm so thankful that I listened to that small still voice that beckoned me to turn around and go back in...

Listening

The value of having someone listen to you and your story was really shown to me one day when I was visiting at the hospital in my chaplain role and entered the room of an elderly gentleman. He invited me in and offered for me to take a seat, which I did. He then started to talk and talk and talk.

He poured out his life story and gave commentary around each subject in great detail. After around fifteen minutes of not getting a word in I realised he was a chronic over-talker. At that point I began to have that internal struggle again and I found myself starting to drift off in my own thoughts.

I had a sense that it was important to stay and listen to him, really listen and to actively stay with him while being fully present. So, for the next 45 minutes, I didn't say anything. I just listened intently, being genuinely interested in what he was saying. It wasn't easy but I put everything into it like it was the most important thing I could be doing in that moment. I will never forget what happened next...

After an hour of solidly listening to this gentleman, he suddenly stopped. He looked at me and said:

"No one has ever listened to me like that before."

It brings tears to my eyes to realise what a difference that had made for him. He went on to say that he knew that he was an over talker and that everyone that he tries to talk to switches off and tries to get him to stop talking. He told me with tears in his eyes how wonderful it was to have someone listen to him, really listen.

I left his room feeling drained but elated that I had managed to stay with him. Again - this was actually a gift *he gave to me*, for me to realise what it means to someone to not only feel listened to but to *actually feel heard*.

Empathy

One of the wards I worked in as a chaplain was the cancer ward. I worked with women with breast cancer and visited many each day. I got to know quite a lot about what they experienced as I sat with each person in their rooms, hearing their experiences and sitting in multi-disciplinary meetings discussing treatment options.

I remember one day sitting with a lady who was very distressed. To be honest, my first thoughts as she started to share her story was:

"I've heard this story before."

I sat and listened to her but was not really with her. All of a sudden, I remember thinking to myself:

"What am I doing?"

It was like I suddenly came to my senses, and it hit me:

"I have no idea what it's like for this precious person that I am sitting with. I don't know what it is like for her to have this diagnosis, to be in this pain, to feel the feelings that she has."

I realised something had blocked my empathy.

When your empathy is blocked, it's a good indication that you have been triggered by something. In this situation, I was not connecting with her, so in a way, I was protecting myself from feeling her pain.

It could be that:

➪ I was experiencing compassion fatigue, that I had heard so many stories, I simply could not hear one more
➪ I was doing my job but not stepping into the space with the person
➪ the person reminded me of someone I knew, so to protect myself, I didn't connect

It's good to reflect when this happens and see what it is that has caused the trigger. Sometimes having someone to reflect with such as a supervisor can really assist us as we may not see it for ourselves.

I have found that to have true empathy is to imagine for a moment *who* this person is, *what* they are experiencing and *how* they are feeling, and to convey to the person that you are *attempting to understand* what it is like for them.

What is it like to live life in their shoes, to walk the path that they have walked? What was it like for them growing up, did they have a happy childhood? What was their family like, do they have siblings? What were their parents like, do they still see them, are they still alive? Are they married, do they have children, grandchildren?

What are their past experiences with cancer? What are their fears, what are their dreams? What is it that gives their life meaning? What are their beliefs, their values?

In this moment today, how are they experiencing the world? What are they thinking, feeling? What is it like to be them in this moment with all that is happening to them and around them?

I realised that day how easy it would be to think that I knew what it was like for her. I had seen so many women in her situation, but on that occasion, it really hit me that I had *no idea* what it was like for her.

Her situation, in fact, everyone's situation is unique. Even if they have the same illness, the impact on her and how she was personally experiencing it is going to be different from everyone else. She has her own thoughts, feelings and disappointments, and she filters them through her *own beliefs* and *that* which gives her life meaning.

How arrogant of me to even begin to think I knew what it was like for her to experience this - that I had heard the 'story' before!

I learnt such a valuable lesson that day about what real empathy is: to communicate that I am simply trying to begin to imagine for a moment what it might be like for her to experience this; to attempt to sit with her in her pain; to listen, to be fully present and to really be with her.

Background to Support and Action Process Model

You may have found yourself in a position where you are with someone, and they're going through a difficult time, and you really want to help them. The problem is that you just don't know what to say or what to do. I think we can all experience this at times.

I have noticed that when people are wanting to support someone, they feel as though they have to try and do something to make the person feel better. Or try and fix the problem. Or do something practical to help the person.

There seems to be a real emphasis on *doing* something; we seem compelled to want to move straight to *action*. We ask or think:

"What can I *do* to help?"

This can lead to the person being helped practically but they may not feel supported emotionally.

I developed a model to assist people to feel more confident to approach a person that needs support. The model can be used to ensure that people feel equipped, regardless of their role or relationship with the person needing support.

The Support and Action Process Model can also be used to assist people to consider if the person may need or want emotional support *before* jumping into action.

When we are overcome by the feelings of helplessness and inadequacy, we can sometimes decide to just avoid the person in need. Or, we might feel a need to *do something practical*.

We may lack confidence and be concerned that if we offer support, we will make the situation even worse.

Hopefully, by using this model, you will feel much more confident to offer emotional support to others, and know when to transition to action, all while keeping appropriate boundaries.

SUPPORT AND ACTION PROCESS MODEL

The Support and Action Process Model is a guideline to follow, providing a clear way to offer emotional support to people before moving to action and offering practical assistance.

The model is like a clock face: you can move around the circle and follow the steps as you do so.

The model covers:

⇨ your preparation
⇨ how to provide emotional support
⇨ how to transition to rational thought
⇨ how to transition into action, offering practical assistance

The model finishes off with the importance of you reflecting on the time with the person and receiving support yourself.

While this model is specifically designed to be used by chaplains, it can be used by anyone wanting to provide emotional and practical support to others.

For supervisors and mentors, the model serves as a reminder to not move too quickly to action but to be mindful of the importance of also offering emotional support.

This model is a good one to learn and have ready to use at any time. We never know when we will encounter someone who looks to us for assistance.

Rather than it simply being a skill we learn, my hope is that when people regularly use this model, *they themselves* will be transformed, with the model becoming part of *who they are* so they eventually just intuitively respond to people in this way.

Support & Action Process Model

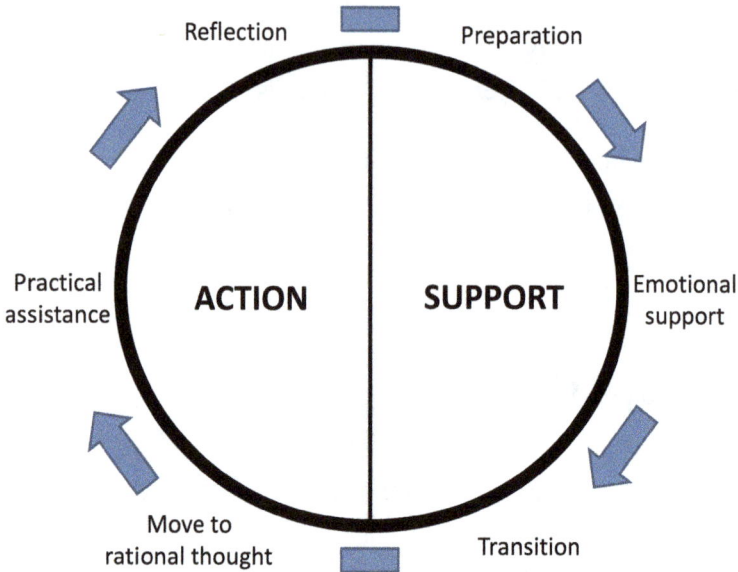

© Susan Marcuccio 2016

USING THE SUPPORT AND ACTION PROCESS MODEL

⇨ PREPARATION

Check your own feelings

In order to use this model, a good habit to get into is to be aware of how you are feeling at any given time. For some people, this is second nature but to others, it can feel strange to have this awareness.

Try it now: how do you feel *right now*? I call it a 'feelings check'. See if you can name a few feelings that you are experiencing right now. For example, you may feel sad or angry or happy or peaceful.

The reason that this is important is so that you notice if your feelings change when you are with the person. If you have advanced warning that you are going to meet with someone or know that you will be seeing them, then you can do a 'feelings check' before you walk in the room or before you meet with them.

It is helpful to notice if you are feeling any strong emotions <u>before</u> you see them as it can be helpful to get yourself into a place where you are feeling as calm as possible so you don't bring strong emotions into the room with you. So, either <u>before</u> you approach the person or <u>as</u> you approach them, be aware of how you are feeling…

Get a sense of the atmosphere

To go one step further, when you enter a room, you can often sense the atmosphere. Sensing the atmosphere can give you some idea of what's going on there.

When we enter the room or the situation, we can be affected by the atmosphere or we can in some way change the atmosphere, so what we bring into the room is important.

For example, we might enter a room feeling happy and full of hope. The room we walk into may be filled with sadness and tension. It's important that we notice the atmosphere.

Often people don't notice this at all, and they think that they suddenly feel sad and tense, but it is actually the atmosphere in the room brought in by one or a number of *other* people.

We can either succumb to the sadness and tension or we can be aware of it and let it inform us as to what may be happening for the people in the room.

We can also sometimes change the atmosphere with how we are feeling as I truly believe we can bring our own happiness and hope into the situation.

Know your role and boundaries

Remind yourself what your role is with the person as this will assist you to have appropriate boundaries. If you are in a professional role, make sure they know your role as well, as this helps the person to be clear about who you are and then they can decide whether to be open with you or not.

Know your boundaries around confidentiality and duty of care issues. If they disclose something to you that needs to be reported, you cannot keep it confidential and must take appropriate action. You may need to communicate this to them.

Follow the policies and procedures of the organisation you are working for. If the person is a family member, friend or colleague, remind *yourself* what the boundaries are with this person. People tend to feel safer with someone that they can see has appropriate boundaries.

Be aware of your aim

It's good to also consider what your aim is. What are you 'hoping for' from this encounter with the person? What is the 'purpose' for you being there with them on this day?

You may say: "I just want to help them or support them," but think a bit deeper:

Do you have a pre-set agenda for being with them?

We often think we don't, but if we dig deeper, we might realise that we do have our 'own agenda' about what we want to happen.

Sometimes, we offer support to another person as a way of meeting a need in ourselves. If that's the case, you may want to discuss this with your supervisor. It's important to always consider what the other person wants or needs from us. Having our own agenda, even if we don't verbally communicate it to the person, can often be picked up by them and then this can sometimes lead to the person feeling unsupported. They could end up feeling like they are a 'project that needs fixing' rather than having someone with them that genuinely cares with no agenda but to be with them and try to be there for them.

Be mindful of what's happening for them and for you

As you can see, we are slowing the process down to be really aware of what's happening and to be more intentional about the support we are providing. Consider for a moment what it might be like for this person to be experiencing this situation at this time. If you are a person of faith, you may like to pray before you enter the room or into the conversation. The idea here is to slow it all down so you are more mindful of what is happening for you and for the other person. Only then will you be ready to begin the process of providing support.

⇨ EMOTIONAL SUPPORT

Being present in the moment

The first part of the process is all about being with the person, fully present in the moment, making a connection and building rapport. It's easy to 'be with someone' but be thinking about 'other things or people' so that actually, in our minds, *we are somewhere else.*

What a gift it is to communicate to someone that they have your *full attention!*

Try getting into the moment now: look around the room you are in and focus on a few items, such as a chair or an object. Really notice where you are. If you are outside, notice a plant or a rock or something similar. You are then suddenly there: *in the moment.*

It's similar when you are <u>with someone</u>: look at them and really see them, be present with them in the moment. Make that connection with them and build rapport so that they trust you. Then, you can *really engage* in meaningful communication.

Some people won't want to share how they are feeling, so don't force it, just give them the opportunity to share if they want to. My experience has been that most people, if they feel safe enough, will share - especially if they can do it 'at their own pace'.

Engage in meaningful communication

Once you have built rapport with the person and you are there with them in the moment, listen to the person and really hear what they are saying or what they are *not saying.* Communication is so much more than just what a person says - we communicate with our body language, the tone in our voice and even just with our presence. It's about letting the person know that you are with them and that they are not alone, either by the demonstration of your care for them or by speaking it out, if appropriate.

In this part of the process, we allow the person to share if they want to without us interrupting or trying to lead the conversation in a specific direction. Try to just reflect what the person says back to them, such as:

➭ "You are finding this difficult."
➭ "You're feeling overwhelmed."

This lets the person know that you have heard them and can also help validate how they are feeling. Avoid sharing too much of your own story, even if it's similar, as it can take the focus off the other person.

Keep listening and showing empathy. Empathy is when you convey to the person that you are attempting to understand what it might be like for them to be experiencing this situation in this moment. Try not to show judgement either by your words or body language otherwise the person may shut down and put up a wall. Even if you don't agree with the person, telling someone that they are wrong or that there is something wrong with them can bring guilt or shame and the person may feel like hiding from you emotionally.

As much as possible, try and stay impartial as if you get too involved in their story, you can lose your ability to be objective. Show empathy but try not to take sides by colluding with them. Colluding is when we only see the situation from their perspective and start to agree with them. It can be more helpful to just respond with something like:

"I hear you," rather than: "Yes, I agree."

We are usually much more of a help if we stay objective as we can see a broader perspective which may assist the person at some point. Avoid defending a particular perspective or person as this draws us into the story where we might be less effective, especially if we are drawn into *taking a side*.

Consider the person's worldview

We all try and explain to ourselves what's happening in the world and what's happening to us as individuals by developing an *assumptive worldview*. It's the way that we 'assume the world to be' even if it's not. An 'assumptive worldview' enables people to feel safe in the world. The person you are supporting will have a particular way that they see the world and they will 'hang on to that' to keep feeling safe.

When we face a difficult situation or something major happens to us, the very things that we believe and that keep us safe may be challenged. It's important that we give the person space to express this and for us to listen and provide support as they try and get back to a place of safety. Their safety zone will be the place where *what they believe* makes sense again. Or, in some cases, a person may find themselves *changing what they believe* to fit their new circumstances.

It's a very vulnerable place to be when we are trying to make sense of the world and what is happening *around us* and *to us*, so just being there with a person can be so helpful. Again, just listen and if needed, reply but don't give in to the temptation to try and fix it or to explain it away by using a platitude. Examples of platitudes are:

➪ *"Everything happens for a reason."*
➪ *"It could be worse."*

Platitudes can be a way of trying to justify why something has happened. Whilst we may say them to others (and even to ourselves) to offer reassurance or provide an explanation, they are rarely helpful. If you find you want to say something, you could instead try using phrases such as:

➪ *"What is that like?"*
➪ *"I'm here with you."*

Check how you are feeling

Be aware how you are feeling now that you are in the room or in the space with the person. Have you noticed any change in your emotions? If you have, then it may be *transference* of feelings from the other person to you. That is, you may be sensing the feelings that they have brought into the room or how they are feeling right now.

Checking how you feel is a skill that takes time to develop, so practice noticing when your feelings change and try to discern if they are *your feelings* or if you are picking up *their feelings*. This can be a good way to sense where the other person is at and how they are feeling without actually asking them. Having the ability to do this might be described as *advanced empathy*.

While it is important to be authentic and to *feel with* the person, we are often the most valuable when we are aware of our own feelings and are able to stay calm and present with the person without being overcome by our own emotions.

Validation of their emotions

In summary, the first part of the process (the emotional support section) is about really being with the person, hearing and seeing them and helping them to feel validated in the emotions they may be feeling.

Don't underestimate how important it is for a person to have their feelings acknowledged - to be able to express those feelings and not have them shut down.

It's not easy to stay with a person when they are feeling such emotional pain. So, if you are attempting this: well done – it is *not easy*. Watch their body language as well as your own, as this will also give some clues as to what's happening for them and for you in the moment.

Again, we are slowing it down to be more mindful of what is really going on here. So, providing emotional support is really just *being with* a person, helping them know that they are not alone and allowing them to have their feelings heard and validated.

⇨ TRANSITION

Look out for the shift

Eventually you will notice that the person will sigh or there will be some silence. You will sense a shift: the person has had the chance to share and be heard and feels emotionally supported. They are then ready to consider what they need to do, and we are ready to move to the action stage of the process, to transition from support to action.

Reflective Summary

You may want to end this section by sharing a reflective summary as part of the transition. A reflective summary is a statement that summarises what they have communicated to you. For example:

"It sounds like it's been such a difficult time… Thank you for sharing some of your experience with me."

⇨ PROVIDING PRACTICAL ASSISTANCE

Moving from feelings to rational thought

The second part of the process is all about continuing the support but moving to the action stage. Once a person has shared their feelings, they can often move to thinking more rationally. It's very hard to think straight when you are overcome with emotion.

We also want to assist the person to be able to get to a stage where they can bring down their emotions before we leave them. Moving to the practical stage helps with this.

They may not need any practical assistance, they may have just wanted some emotional support, so be sensitive to this and again, don't force it.

Empower the person

If they are looking for practical assistance, empower them to look at what they need. This gives people dignity and helps them to find their own solutions.

Don't assume you know what they need or what is going to help them. It's often not what we think. They may have been in this situation before and already know what they need to do. Let them come up with any options they may have and to tap into their own support systems.

Know what you can offer

Check where the person is at, what they are now planning to do and what they are needing or wanting. Know what it is that you can offer the person in your role, keeping appropriate boundaries and knowing what other referrals options are available or required.

⇨ REFLECTION

Process your own emotions

After the encounter with the person, take some time to reflect and be aware of how you are feeling. Notice if you find that something about the time with them has really affected you and you need to talk with someone about it, such as your supervisor or someone who is a support to you.

It's important to take the time to reflect on the encounters that we have with people so we can process them and make sure that we are not carrying around baggage or unprocessed emotions.

Your own support, best practice and learning

When you see your supervisor, you may want to do some further reflection in the session with them to get your own support, ensure best practice and to learn from it.

The Support and Action Process Model in summary:

➡ **Preparation**

- O Check your own feelings
- O Get a sense of the atmosphere
- O Know your role and boundaries
- O Be aware of your aim
- O Be mindful of what is happening for them and for you

➡ **Emotional Support**

- O Be present in the moment
- O Engage in meaningful communication
- O Consider the person's worldview
- O Check how you are feeling
- O Validate their emotions

➡ **Transition**

- O Look out for the shift
- O Reflective summary

➡ **Practical Assistance**

- O Move from feelings to rational thought
- O Empower the person
- O Know what you can offer

➡ **Reflection**

- O Process your own emotions
- O Your own support, best practice and learning

CHAPTER THREE

UNWRAPPING THE GIFT
OF SUPERVISION

Find that space
Lean in
Be heard
Be seen
Be held
Be yourself

Lift your eyes
See more clearly
Above and beyond
A broader view
See things differently
Gain clarity and perspective

Vision and values
Purpose and passion
Be intentional
Be transformed
Be equipped
Be your best self

I love presents, giving them and receiving them: it's one of my love languages. So, a visual image I have for supervision is that it is a gift, a present to be unwrapped. I can't even begin to tell you what it was like for me when I unwrapped supervision for myself. I found the most amazing gift.

Since then, I have realised there are so many layers to this gift and just as I take one layer of wrapping paper off and find a gift, I realise there is another layer to unwrap. My hope is that you will also take hold of the gift of supervision and start to unwrap it for yourself. If you have already discovered this amazing gift, then perhaps you will discover some more layers!

THREE RINGED MODEL

People often ask me the question: *What is supervision*? It's a great question and one you may also be asking. Rather than simply trying to explain what supervision is in words, I decided to create the *Three Ringed Model* - a model that would help people to clearly understand what supervision is and what the main focus is.

The three ringed model is a visual picture that shows that the main focus of supervision is a person's work life or, put another way, their profession, vocation, business or ministry. It also shows that a person's work life overlaps with their personal life and their spiritual life.

This model shows that in order for supervision to be holistic, we work in the overlap between work life and personal life but don't go so far that it becomes counselling or therapy. It also shows that we work in the overlap between a person's work life and spiritual life, but don't go so far that it becomes spiritual direction or takes the place of a person's faith community (if they have one).

Another question I am often asked is: *How is supervision different to other types of support?* The 'Three Ringed Model' clearly shows that supervision differs from other types of support by having a clear focus on your work life but also importantly considers the overlap with your personal life and your spiritual life.

The three ringed model can be used by anyone wanting to understand what supervision is and how it fits in with other kinds of support for themselves or to be able to explain it to others.

It can be used by supervisors in a supervision session as a model to explain the holistic nature of supervision; it can be used as a reflective tool; and, it can also be used as the basis for an activity for personal, professional and spiritual growth.

In summary, the 'Three Ringed Model' can be used by:

➡ Anyone, as a model to explain what supervision is
➡ Supervisors, mentors or chaplains as a personal, professional and spiritual tool
➡ Supervisors to assist a supervisee to choose a topic to look at in supervision
➡ Supervisors as a reflective tool to reflect on a supervision session

THREE RINGED MODEL

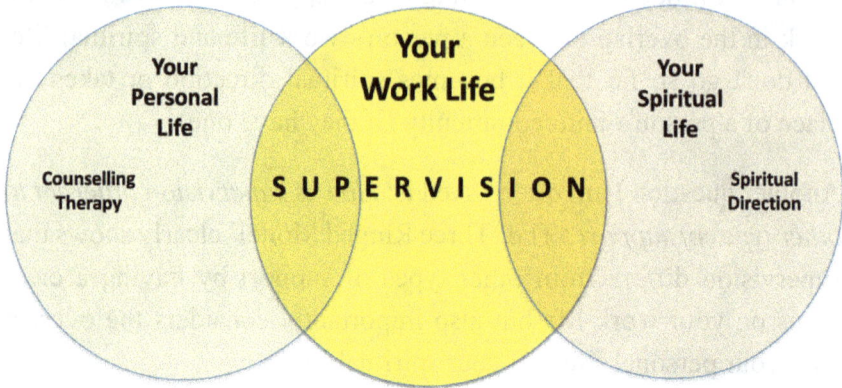

Your Personal Life

Your Work Life

Your Spiritual Life

Counselling Therapy

S U P E R V I S I O N

Spiritual Direction

© Susan Marcuccio 2013

I tend to use this model in the first session I have with a new supervisee. If they are new to supervision, it can give a really clear picture of what supervision is and what the focus of it is. It can sometimes be helpful for them to actually draw the model and then they can refer back to it after the session.

I think the model gives real clarity to what supervision is and isn't. It also helps those who have had supervision before to know how I approach supervision and helps the supervisee to consider what parts of the model they are interested in working in.

The model can also be helpful for supervisors to use to reflect on their supervision sessions and to see where they worked with a supervisee. Are they spending all their time in the overlap between personal and work and never going into the spiritual and work overlap?

Personal Life	Work Life	Spiritual Life
This is your home life, your family, friends, your life outside of your work, your personal life.	This is the focus of supervision. It relates to your work, your profession, your ministry, or your business.	This represents what gives your life meaning, your beliefs, values, what is important to you. Also, how you out-work what you believe.
What's happening in your personal life can affect your work life. What's happening in your work can have an effect on your personal life.	Supervision has a focus on who you are, as well as what you do. It provides support, assists with ensuring best practice and provides a safe, confidential, brave space for engaging in skills training and transformational learning.	Your spiritual life informs the way you approach and undertake your work. What happens in your work can also affect your spiritual life.
In supervision, we look at the cross over between your personal life and work life. How you transition from home to work/work to home, your holistic wellness/wellbeing. We create an environment for you to journey to become your authentic integrated self.	We enter into the process of supervision using a variety of models and tools, using case studies or experiences from within your work context or around your profession. We engage in reflective practice and as we explore different perspectives, greater clarity emerges.	In supervision, we look at the cross over between your spiritual life and your work life. We explore your unique purpose, your beliefs, values, what gives your life meaning, your passion and how all this is congruent with your work.
For additional support for your personal life, you could access counselling or therapy, see GP for referral to a psychologist, engage a life coach or personal mentor.	For additional support for your work life, you could undertake coaching or mentoring for a specific purpose or to gain insight from a master of your craft.	For additional support for your spiritual life, you could engage with a spiritual director or connect with a faith community consistent with your spiritual beliefs.

Supervisors, mentors and chaplains can use the Three Ringed Model when they are working with someone who wants to look at their life holistically as they consider their goals for their personal, professional and spiritual lives.

THE RINGS IN THE 'THREE RINGED MODEL'

In order to understand the Three Ringed Model, I will now break it down into the three rings, to gain more clarity on *each ring*:

The middle ring (work life): main focus of supervision

The circle in the middle is what we will call your work life. This refers to your work, your profession, your vocation, your business or your ministry. This sits at the very centre and is the primary focus of supervision.

Supervision has a focus on *who you are* in your work, as well as *what you do* in your work.

Supervision provides support for you in your work, assists with ensuring best practice in your profession and provides a safe, confidential space for engaging in skills training and transformational learning.

We enter into the process of supervision using a variety of models and tools, using case studies or experiences from within your work context or around your profession.

In supervision, we are engaging in reflective practice. As we explore different perspectives, *greater clarity emerges.*

For additional support for your work life, you could undertake coaching or mentoring for a specific purpose or to gain insight from a master of your craft.

The left ring (personal life): overlaps with a person's work life

The circle to the left is what we will call your personal life and it overlaps with your work life. In supervision, we work primarily with your work life but in order for it to be holistic, we need to also take into account what's happening in your personal life.

Supervision enables you to have a confidential supportive space to share what is happening in your world without fear of judgement. We look at areas like self-care, your work/life balance, your stress levels, avoiding burnout, and your overall holistic wellness.

We look at how you transition from work to home and from home to work, being very aware that what's happening in your personal life can have an effect on the way you do your work and what's happening in your work can have an impact on your personal life.

We work in the area of the crossover, being careful not to venture *across the boundary* into counselling or giving medical advice. It is the role of the supervisor to ensure that this boundary is not crossed and when necessary, to make a referral to a counsellor or a doctor.

On occasion, what's happening in a person's personal life is dominating, such as a significant loss or life event. It is important that we are flexible enough to realise that, *at this time*, the person may need more support than anything else and that is what we could offer them.

We can touch on how a person's personal life may be affecting their work life but *be sensitive* to the persons needs at this time. Offer support within the boundaries of your role.

I find that when people don't have regular supervision or mentoring (or have none at all), they come to supervision *only when* they have a personal crisis in their life, and then the focus is continually on their personal life and tends to be reactionary rather than preventative.

If over time, this continued to happen, then it may be good to have a conversation around putting in place <u>regular</u> supervision or mentoring.

Personal Life/Work Life

On occasion, what's happening in a person's personal life is dominating, such as a significant loss, or life event or personal life/work life is the area the person would like to focus on.

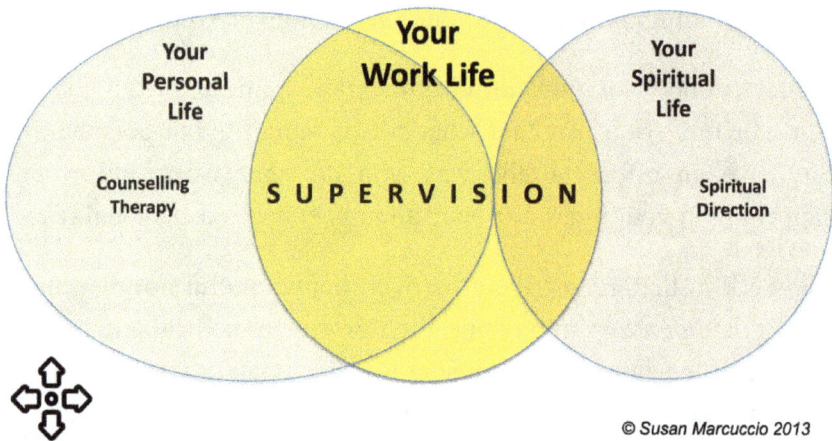

© Susan Marcuccio 2013

The right ring (spiritual life): overlaps with a person's work life

The circle on the right we will call your spiritual life. Supervision works also in the crossover between your work life and your spiritual life. When I say spiritual life, I'm referring to your beliefs, your values, your worldview, the things that are important to you, what gives your life meaning.

Spirituality also refers to how you 'outwork' what you believe, and how all this is congruent with your work. These are all important parts of your life and supervision would not be holistic without taking these into consideration. Your spiritual life informs the way you do your work, and what's happening in your work can influence aspects of your spiritual life.

In supervision, we work in the area of the crossover, being careful not to *cross the boundary* into spiritual direction or to take the place of your own faith or spiritual community (if you have one). It is the role of the supervisor to ensure that this boundary is not crossed.

For additional support for your spiritual life, you could engage with a spiritual director or connect with a faith community consistent with your spiritual beliefs.

Work Life/Spiritual Life

On occasion, what's happening in a person's spiritual life is dominating, such as a crisis of faith or spiritual distress or work life/spiritual life is the area the person would like to focus on.

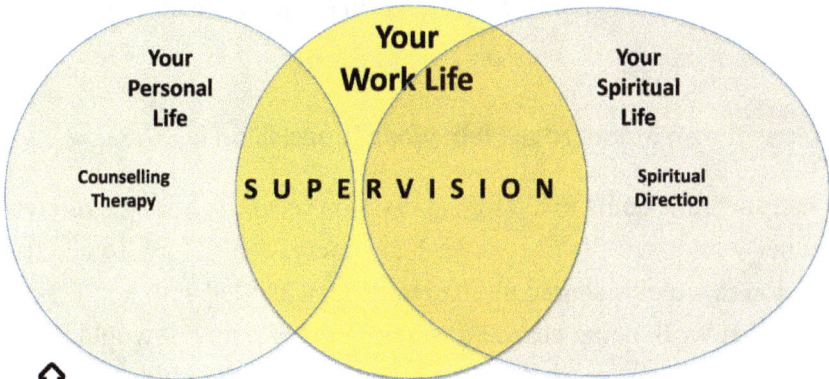

© Susan Marcuccio 2013

When a significant event has happened, a person may be in a vulnerable place, as what they believe may be challenged, and they may need a safe place to discuss and explore this. So, be sensitive to what the person needs on the day. Provide support and be careful not to bring in your own agenda but simply 'hold the space' for them to work through this difficult place to be in.

You can touch on how this is affecting their work if it's appropriate and it's what the person wants to focus on. Supervision and mentoring can be a very appropriate place to discuss what's happening in a person's spiritual life but stay within the boundary of your role and refer if needed.

WAYS TO USE THE 'THREE RINGED MODEL'

The 'Three Ringed Model' can be used in numbers of ways:

- ➡ To use it as a model to explain what supervision is
- ➡ To assist a supervisee to choose a topic to look at in supervision
- ➡ As a reflective tool to reflect on a supervision session
- ➡ To use it as a personal, professional and spiritual tool

To use it as a model to explain what supervision is

I had someone come to me for supervision recently. She was referred by her workplace. Having never had supervision before, in our first session together, I shared the 'Three Ringed Model' with her. I spoke about her work being central to supervision and how it would be the main focus in our sessions. She looked relieved and said:

"That's wonderful news as I feel like I have good support personally by my family and friends and I have a psychologist that I have seen a few times when I've needed it. I have people that are supporting me spiritually, I have a spiritual mentor and have a supportive faith community. The part that is missing is confidential support for my work life. A place to go to help me grow and develop in my profession, and to make sure I'm being the best that I can be in my role."

She went on to say that she loved that supervision brought it all together and would support her in her work and also her work/life balance in the crossover between her personal life and her work life. Supervision also took into consideration what was important to her, her beliefs, her values and how that informed her work in the crossover between her work life and her spiritual life.

I thought that her observations summed up supervision so well. It's the *missing piece of support* for so many. You may have seen a Guidance Counsellor at school or had support when you studied in your chosen field but since then, you may have really been on your own in regards to your work and your profession.

While you might have a wonderful supportive workplace, having a supervisor who is trained to assist you to work through any challenges, to know more about yourself and why you respond the way you do in certain circumstances, is vital for your own personal and professional growth and development.

Supervision also means that you can work some of these things out with someone <u>outside</u> of your workplace. This is beneficial, as sometimes we are reluctant to share things with those at work, as we can feel concerned that it might impact on our job. By engaging in supervision, we can do our internal processing away from our work. Then, having looked at new perspectives with our supervisor, we can be ready for discussions in our workplace.

Having someone meet with you on a monthly basis to see how you're going in your work; making sure you are doing something you love and that you are being stretched and developed; living in a way that is holistically healthy and really thriving – all make up the essence of what supervision is.

To assist a supervisee to choose a topic to look at in supervision

Explaining the 'Three Ringed Model' to someone can really assist them to choose what they would like to discuss in supervision. You can ask them to look at a list (such as the one below) and to choose an area that they would like to work on in the supervision session:

Here are some options for using this model:

Personal Life/ Work Life	Work Life	Work Life/ Spiritual Life
Self-care	Case studies	Values/core values
Work/life balance	Work challenges	Spiritual/work challenges
Personal issues affecting work	Support	Worldview
Work issues affecting home	Best practice	Meaning making
Stress and burn out	Skill development	Beliefs
Home/work transition	Transformational learning	Theological reflection

To use it as a reflective tool

By using the 'Three Ringed Model,' a supervisor can reflect on a supervision session and see where they did most of the work. Was it just on work life or was it on their personal life/work life or work life/spiritual life?

I was working with a supervisor who realised that nearly all their interactions with their supervisees were in the personal life/work life area with only some interactions focusing on *just their work life*. With the aid of this model as a reflective tool, the supervisor was able to clearly see what was happening and decided to pay more attention to the work life and work life/spiritual life areas of his supervisees.

Looking at what people had brought to supervision through the lens of this model meant that the scope of the supervision sessions was able to be broadened while still ensuring that supervisees were the ones making the choices about which areas to concentrate on.

It also ensured that the supervision space was able to become more holistic as there was consideration from multiple perspectives including a person's work life, personal life and spiritual life, within the boundaries of supervision.

To use it as a personal, professional and spiritual tool

When a supervisee would like to use a supervision session to set goals for what they want to achieve and/or who they want to be, then the 'Three Ringed Model' can be used as a guide to look at each area of a person's life. It can also inform the discussion around how supervision or mentoring can assist with this.

The 'Three Ringed Model' can be used by anyone but if used in the context of supervision, the focus is the person's *work life* and the *crossover* with personal life and spiritual life.

If used outside of these areas of the person's life, we can problem solve with the supervisee to determine who might be best to assist them with what is happening for them. Engaging a coach or mentor could be ideal in this situation.

To use the 'Three Ringed Model' as a personal, professional and spiritual tool, follow these steps:

Step One: Ask the person to draw the "Three Ringed Model." In the left ring write *Personal Life*, in the middle ring write *Work Life*, and in the right ring write *Spiritual Life*.

Step Two: Under each of the circles, ask them to list goals they have for each area of their lives. The goals will be in two parts: who they want TO BE and what they want TO DO.

Step Three: Ask the person to reflect on what they have written and what they notice. You don't need to comment too much - it's just interesting to see what emerges. There may be themes that you both notice or crossovers between the different areas. There could also be one area that has featured more than others which will give some indication as to where the person wants growth and development.

It is deliberately divided into the two sections (TO BE and TO DO) as most people, when they write goals, just focus on what they want to do and achieve. It can be helpful for the person to also consider who they 'want to be'. This often helps people to see new perspectives around their learning and goals.

Step Four: Ask the person to consider who can assist them with their goals. If you are with them in a supervision session, then together, consider which ones could be covered in future sessions. This can be really helpful to assist in developing the overall contract with your supervisee on how you would like to work collaboratively on their goals and introduces a framework to work with.

© Susan Marcuccio 2013

Personal Life Goals		Work Life Goals		Spiritual Life Goals	
TO BE	TO DO	TO BE	TO DO	TO BE	TO DO

Super-Vision

Hopefully, the 'Three Ringed Model' has given you more clarity around what supervision is, and you may now feel as though you have the gift in your hand. Perhaps you have just taken off the first layer of wrapping paper and it is becoming clearer.

People often ask me about the term 'supervision' as it is used in many different contexts. I like to think of supervision as SUPER-VISION!

'Super-vision' is such a great word for highlighting what we actually do in supervision:

SUPER: 'above and beyond'

VISION: 'to see; a view'

SUPER-VISION: 'to see; a view; above and beyond'

Supervision: an intentional space to explore and see above and beyond what we currently see. To gain a broader view, to see from a different perspective, to have greater clarity - to see more clearly. To see things differently.

We can so easily be stuck in our own way of thinking and seeing the world. SUPER-VISION is what you actually get in supervision.

What if we were all more open to seeing NEW PERSPECTIVES?? Supervision is such a wonderful way to do that: it gives us an opportunity to stop and look at things differently; to have our thinking stretched beyond what we think we know; to see things from another perspective.

I hope you can see why I think it is such a gift!

Professional Supervision

The type of supervision that I am referring to in this chapter and throughout *New Perspectives in Supervision* is 'Professional Supervision' which differs from other types of supervision.

Your current association with the word 'supervision' may be to relate it to 'management' or 'responsibility', as in 'being supervised or line-managed'. This is a reasonable assumption as the term 'supervision' is used a lot in management, for example with new or inexperienced staff or those lower down the chain of hierarchy.

'Managerial supervision' does happen in some professions and workplaces but that's not the type of supervision I am referring to here. 'Professional Supervision' is very different from being supervised by a line-manager or more experienced staff member.

Your professional supervisor is usually someone outside of your workplace. This is a key point, as having someone who is not involved in your organisation or workplace gives you freedom to be able to discuss work-related things without being concerned that it will affect your job.

Professional supervision *does* relate to your job (your work life) even though your supervisor might not have the same professional skills as you. It's not actually necessary for a professional supervisor to have the same or even related clinical or business skills as their supervisees in order to be effective in their role.

Having said that, a professional supervisor will be *interested* in what you do at work and is someone who will be able to assist you to create a place where you can be accountable, to help you 'stay on track' in your *work life*.

Credentials of a Professional Supervisor

'Professional Supervision' is usually undertaken with someone who is trained in the *Profession of Supervision* – someone who was required to complete a certain amount of theory and practice hours before being recognised as a 'Professional Supervisor'.

In addition to their training, 'Professional Supervisors' must engage in their <u>own</u> supervision.

Some professional supervisors use the term 'Recognised' before their title to indicate that they are maintaining a minimum standard of regular professional development and engaging in their own supervision.

Other Titles and Information about Supervision

While 'Professional Supervision' is the overarching term used, it can be broken down into streams which include: 'Clinical Supervision' for those in clinical roles and 'Pastoral Supervision' which is for people of faith. Many other streams of 'Professional Supervision' are emerging such as in education and other business areas.

Ideally, people meet with their supervisor for supervision once a month or at least once every three months to get the most out of supervision. Sessions can be conducted face to face or online, and in some cases, by phone.

Supervision is mandatory or highly recommended in most of the helping professions which is wonderful as organisations are seeing the many benefits of having their staff and volunteers engaging in supervision.

Here are some of the many benefits of engaging in supervision:

- ➪ Receive care and support
- ➪ Encourages holistic health
- ➪ Better understanding of yourself & others
- ➪ See new perspectives
- ➪ Helps you to flourish in your role
- ➪ Connects you to your calling and purpose
- ➪ Assists in living an authentic life
- ➪ A place to process your emotions and life events
- ➪ Grow personally and professionally
- ➪ Deal with offences/being offended
- ➪ A place to be honest about your struggles
- ➪ Accountability
- ➪ Keeps you and others safe

The strengths and unique nature of supervision:

- ➪ Facilitated by a trained professional supervisor
- ➪ A safe/brave confidential space with clear boundaries
- ➪ Holistic approach with a focus on your work/profession
- ➪ Provides support/learning/best practice
- ➪ Utilises supervision models/tools/processes
- ➪ Partakes in theological reflection for pastoral supervision
- ➪ Engages in reflective practice
- ➪ Assists in finding purpose/passion/calling
- ➪ Gain perspective – greater clarity
- ➪ Identifies values/assumptions/beliefs
- ➪ Self-care strategies in place with follow up
- ➪ Finding your authentic self
- ➪ Recognises transference & counter transference
- ➪ Individual or group supervision opportunities

What we do in supervision:

- ⇨ Engage in reflective practice
- ⇨ Get support and encouragement
- ⇨ Consider case studies
- ⇨ Reflect on work practices and experiences
- ⇨ Understand emotional boundaries
- ⇨ Develop awareness of transference & countertransference
- ⇨ Explore purpose & passion
- ⇨ Gain clarity around calling
- ⇨ Discover our authentic self
- ⇨ Utilise creative methods
- ⇨ Use images & metaphors
- ⇨ Explore short and long term goals
- ⇨ Maintain health and wellbeing
- ⇨ Gain broader perspectives
- ⇨ Develop a greater understanding of the impact of work
- ⇨ Engage in skills training and transformational learning

While supervision is now my main profession, I wanted to also share about chaplaincy and mentoring as they have both played such an important role in my life.

The Heart of Chaplaincy

I love chaplaincy because it is such a wonderful expression of kindness, caring, showing support and helping people to see that they are not alone, at least not *in that moment*. To be a chaplain is to be with someone in their time of need, to give comfort, to walk along side.

We all have times in our lives, whether we admit it or not, when we need others. It is such a sign of strength to ask for help and it also gives others permission to ask for help when they need it. We really do connect with people at the point of vulnerability.

I love that chaplains always look to empower, to help people tap into their own resources. Chaplaincy is about showing respect and not judging others. Chaplains are everywhere, in prisons, schools, hospitals, aged care facilities, shopping centres, communities, disaster settings; really wherever there are people, there can be a chaplain.

I think I will always want to be involved in chaplaincy as it is in my heart. I cannot stand the thought of people suffering alone. I know that there are so many people in the world who care deeply and would just love to be a support to someone. I love that chaplaincy connects these two groups of people.

Maybe you would love to be there for others? If yes, then it's not too late to get trained as a chaplain and to be there for those that you have *on your heart.*

The Need for Mentors

Imagine if we all had someone who was further along the road than us that would come along side us for a season and champion us along. For us to learn from, to be inspired by and to pick us up when we fall.

I always try and see who is around me, who I can learn from, either from afar or, when I have the opportunity, up close. To have those people in my life that will have my back, speak up for me and help me to be all I was created for.

I also look for those that *I can champion*, to believe in and to do what I can to open doors and give those people opportunities.

I always look around and try to offer a word of encouragement to those I can, as I know what a difference it can make to feel as though someone believes in you. How wonderful it would be if we all *had* a mentor and then we all *were* a mentor for someone else.

You could also consider training as a Professional Mentor as many people now choose to do this as part of their role or even their main profession.

If you don't currently have a mentor, I really encourage you to look for one. I believe it will catapult you forward into your purpose and your calling. Why would you try and do it alone?

The Privilege of Being a Supervisor

Sitting with people in supervision as a supervisor is the most amazing privilege. I have learnt so much from those I supervise. The incredible people who in their role: visit people in prison; be with people who are dying; sit with people in the gutter; work with those who find themselves homeless; work tirelessly in aged care facilities; spend time with troubled youth; the list could go on and on…

The people I supervise are all champions. I am indeed blessed to walk alongside them for a time. How wonderful that I can assist them to stay holistically healthy, to see things from new perspectives, to help them see what an incredible difference they are making.

I have also learnt so much from providing supervision to those in leadership positions, who often don't have anyone to talk to about the challenges they are facing. I am in awe of these people who give so much of their lives for others, often without thanks or consideration about how hard it is to deal in so much complexity on a daily basis.

As a supervisor, I also supervise people from all different faiths and denominations which means I get a unique snapshot into what's happening in these areas *across the board*. This has taught me a lot by broadening my view and also learning about different language and terminology as well as the beliefs that others hold.

What an incredible privilege it is to be in the role of a supervisor. Perhaps it's a role you also may consider? I'm sure *you too* would see what a gift supervision really is to so many...

CHAPTER FOUR

TRUSTING THE PROCESS
OF SUPERVISION

Trust the process
Step in and enter
Agree together
Be clear on focus
Know what you want
Don't be distracted

Be brave
Be courageous
Jump in
Have a go
Look around
See new perspectives

Stay in the process
Allow new things to emerge
Gain clarity
Be transformed
Move to action
Take flight

Story and Process

People often talk about the *process* of supervision without really understanding what *process* means or why it's an important part of supervision. In this chapter, I will use several models to explain what I mean when I talk about 'the process of supervision'.

To begin our understanding of the process of supervision, let's look at a key phrase used by professional supervisors:

➡ ENTERING THE PROCESS OF SUPERVISION

The process of supervision starts with the supervisor *listening* to the supervisee's story. By story, we are referring to an *experience* that the supervisee has had. The supervisee brings this story to supervision, to discuss with the supervisor.

To *enter* the process of supervision, the supervisor and the supervisee take time in the first part of the session to deliberately talk about the steps they will take, *together*, within the supervision session. These steps (the process) enable the supervisor and the supervisee to get to the end of the session having achieved what they both set out to do.

Having a process gives the supervisor a road map to follow, helping them to move through each step with the supervisee. At each step, an *element* of supervision is undertaken.

In the next section, I explain the 'Perspective Supervision Process Model' by looking closely at the elements: *experience, listen, contract, focus, reflect, summary, action* and *review*.

Each element is important. It is the inclusion of these elements and the way we progress through the elements, using our road map, that ensures we *enter the process of supervision.*

There is something indescribable that happens when you *enter* the process of supervision: the process seems to do the work for you. So much so, it's almost like, as a supervisor, you are just going along for the ride. This is why we might say:

"Trust the process."

Once you know *how to enter* the process of supervision, you can trust that something profound is likely to happen…

PERSPECTIVE SUPERVISION PROCESS MODEL

The model I created about the process of supervision was inspired by the Cyclical Model of Supervision (Wosket & Page, 2001). I have called my model the 'Perspective Supervision Process Model' as I believe that gaining *new perspectives* is key to the whole process of supervision.

The 'Perspective Supervision Process Model' has been designed to be used by trained supervisors. The model can also be for the purpose of explaining to people what the process of supervision is (the elements) and what happens in a session (the steps).

The model can become the basis of each supervision session: a road map to follow that ensures that the supervision session has all the elements required to *enter the process of supervision.*

I find it helpful to have the printed model with you in a place where it can be seen until you have learnt how to follow the steps in an intuitive way. It might also be helpful to show the printed model to your supervisee so they can see the steps too, particularly if they are resistant to any parts of the process, such as getting in the reflective space.

Refer to the back of this book (p.287) for information on where to access resources (such as the printable version of this model).

Perspective Supervision Process Model

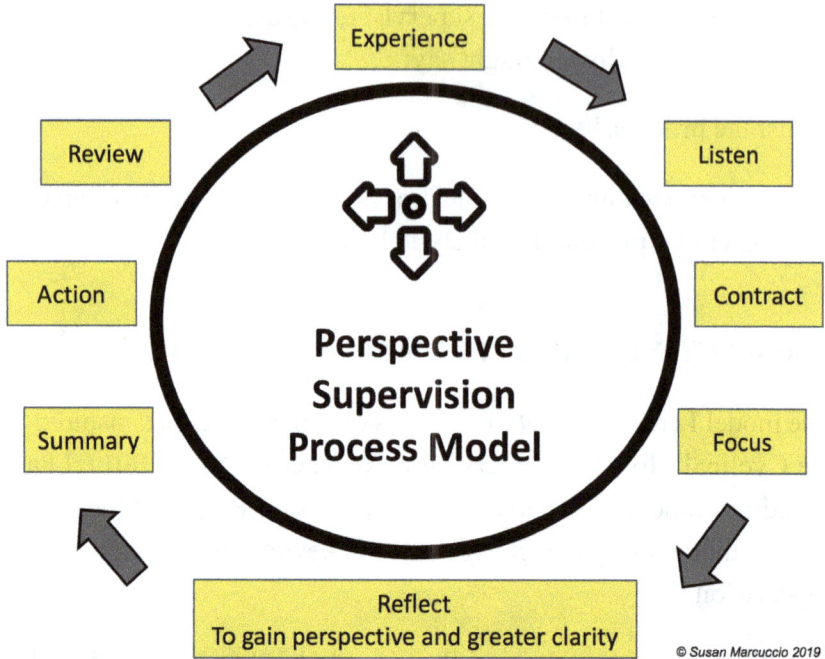

© Susan Marcuccio 2019

Perspective Supervision Process Model Explained

Experience

The first element in the supervision process is: *Experience*. When a person arrives at supervision, whether it's face to face or online, they usually come with a story about an *experience* they have had.

We all have stories that we want to share but often we either don't get the chance or we decide not to share because we don't think it's safe to do so.

It's very important that we honour the story that the person has brought, if they choose to share it with us, while being mindful that we are inviting the person to enter into the process of supervision.

Sometimes people come to supervision because they have had a situational crisis and need someone to talk to that is confidential. Ideally, people enter supervision as a preventative measure, setting up a relationship that will assist them throughout their professional life and then the relationship is already built if a crisis does occur.

Supervision is with someone that is usually outside of the person's life and therefore can offer objective and impartial support. Sometimes, people have either been mandated to come or have been referred or had it suggested to them. Some people decide that it will assist them in their work practice, both personally and professionally.

Regardless of why a person comes to supervision, they bring with them the *experience* that they have gathered over their life as well as the *specific experience* or story that they would like to discuss or reflect on.

They may have questions about a situation they have experienced or feel stuck in a current situation. Initially, people may be unsure about what to bring to supervision, but it usually always stems back to an *experience* (story) they have had or are having that they would like to get clarity on.

The supervisee is bringing their collective *experiences* with them into the room. As a supervisor, I am also bringing my collective *experiences* into the room. So here we are, both sitting in the supervision session with the different *experiences* we have had. At that precise moment, our 'roads of experience' intersect.

We make a time together with the clear purpose of really connecting and entering into a meaningful interaction. It's amazing and such an incredible privilege - to meet together at an appointed time and place for the person to share their *experiences*.

I really think everyone needs to have a supervisor to meet with on a regular basis. I wonder if you have had the opportunity in your life to tell someone about the *experiences* you've had: to have someone who is there - just for you - *how good is that!*

The next element that we move to in the model is: *Listen*.

Listen

As the person arrives at the session, my first role as supervisor is to *listen*. I'm listening to their story, that is, the experience they have decided to bring and share with me on that particular day. I *listen* to what the supervisee is saying, and also what they are not saying.

Hopefully, I have prepared well for the session and find myself feeling calm and peaceful as I *listen*. I work to make sure the person feels welcome; to make it an inviting space; to *listen* for what's happening for the supervisee; to consider what it might be like for them to be here with me.

If you have a supervisee that wants to share something at the start of the session, *listen*, really *listen*. Be with them in the moment. This is the time to validate, to show empathy, to attempt to understand what it might be like for them to have experienced what they have brought with them today.

Try to not be judgmental of what they are sharing, to stop yourself from jumping in with your solutions to their problems. After you have really *listened* to the person and have a good sense of where they are at, it's time for the next element: *Contract*.

Contract

While it is important to be respectful of the story that the person has brought to supervision, it's equally important to move to the next step: *contract.*

The process of supervision started when the supervisee brought their experience to the session and the supervisor listened to their story. However, in order to *enter the process of supervision*, the supervisor and supervisee take the next step together – they *contract.*

The *contract* enables the supervisor and the supervisee to get to the end of the session having achieved what they both set out to do.

Put another way, moving from the step: *'listen'* to the step: *'contract'* ensures that what is happening **is supervision**.

> *"Supervision includes the element of listening;*
> *however, it is **more than** just listening."*

So how do you *contract* for the session?

Each time we meet with a supervisee and start the process of supervision, we need to *contract.* We do this each time, and each session stands alone. The reason we contract each time is due to not necessarily working on the same thing at each session, therefore, each time we meet - we need to *contract.*

At the end of this chapter, I have a section on the 'overall contract' we make with the supervisee. The overall contract is not the same as the element: *Contract* in the model.

[The overall contract is an important part of establishing the supervision relationship and is usually worked on in the first session. It relates to more general aspects of supervision including things that

apply over time, such as when and where sessions will take place and what they are hoping to get from supervision in a more broad sense.]

In this section, when I say *contract*, I am referring to the element: *Contract* as it appears in the process model, that is, the *contract* for the <u>specific session</u> that is occurring on that day.

The *contract* is agreed upon in the first part of the session. To recap, the session starts with listening to the supervisee's story. After they have shared whatever experience they would like to, we work together to set a clear *contract* for that specific session.

Unless the person has made a point to ask me to follow up with them on a specific (previously discussed) issue, I wouldn't usually bring up any questions from past supervision sessions. *There are exceptions to this, and you will get a feel as to whether to check in on a particular issue.*

If there was a duty of care issue, such as mandatory reporting or something that needed follow up from the previous session, then I would raise it. *Duty of care and other related issues are discussed in more detail at the end of the chapter.*

If I was concerned about the supervisee or had other valid concerns relating to a past exchange, I would ask them about it. But generally, unless it's something we agreed together to talk about in each session or from time to time, such as overall goals, I would just listen and then *contract* for the session.

The *contract* is usually verbal. It is basically the 'topic' that we are going to work with <u>on that particular day</u> during the supervision session.

On the next page, I have compiled a list showing some examples of the types of topics that people have brought to me for supervision that have formed the basis of the *contract* for the session.

EXAMPLES OF TOPICS BROUGHT TO SUPERVISION (FORMING BASIS OF CONTRACT)

Engaging in self-care	Better understanding of self	Celebrating positive milestones
Making decisions	Ministry challenges	Gaining new perspectives
Faith questions	Workplace relationships	Organisational challenges
Situational crisis	Unsure how to handle a situation	Conflict with work colleagues
Changing roles	Sorting out priorities	Holistic self-check-in
Dealing with stress	Living authentically	Feeling overloaded at work
Cultural issues	Understanding emotions	Reconnecting with what gives life
Learning goals	Supporting people in crisis	Noticing the sacred moments
Retirement	Raising awareness	Dealing with complaints
Guilt and shame	Feeling overwhelmed	Processing loss and grief
Church leadership	Transference/countertransference	Clarity around purpose and calling
Work/life balance	Parallel processing	Feel like giving up
Vicarious trauma	Expectations v reality	Planning for the future
Boundaries	Concern about burnout	Processing emotions
Lack of confidence	Knowing your values, core values	Dealing with disappointment
Spiritual distress	Forgiveness/unforgiveness	Feeling not good enough/inadequate
Insecurity	Communications skills	Professional goals
Work roles	Cognitive dissonance	Building resilience
Time management	Reflecting on an encounter	Understanding others perspectives
Feeling stuck	Reflecting on being triggered	Worldview shattered or challenged
Debriefing	Lack of job satisfaction	Life changing events

Some of my supervisees are themselves supervisors and while many of the topics listed on the previous page can form part of our supervision-on-supervision sessions, these are some of the other things that supervisors bring to me in supervision:

⇨ Review of a supervision session
⇨ Working with challenging supervisees
⇨ Using supervision tools and models
⇨ Reflecting on specific cases
⇨ Duty of care issues

Once we have contracted together what the supervisee would like to talk about in supervision on that day, we move to the next element: *Focus*.

Focus

The *focus* of the session is where we look at what they would like to get from the session in regards to the topic they have brought to supervision (the contract). Even though the supervisee may have clarity around which topic they would like to look at, there are so many different aspects of the topic we could *focus* on in the session.

We know what the topic is, but **we are not clear on what the supervisee actually wants from the supervision session in regards to the topic.**

If we start to interact with the supervisee on their topic by asking questions at this point, we might start to lead and choose the way that we think the session should go.

For example, a person may come to supervision and want to talk about a situation at work where they felt they had been unfairly treated and someone else got the promotion and not them. So, you start to interact with them by doing the following:

⇨ Ask them to tell you more about it
⇨ Ask them what it was like for them
⇨ You may then ask them what they are going to do about it
⇨ Together look at options

While the examples above may all be helpful at some stage, there are a number of *problems* with interacting in this way *at this point* in the session:

1. We would be trying to assist the supervisee without first having established a clear *focus*
2. The supervisee wouldn't get the opportunity to *keep working through the elements* in the process model, the next one being *'reflect'* where they get to step back and look at the topic from new perspectives
3. The supervisee might follow our suggestions (the suggestions of the supervisor)
4. The supervisee might never get to explore the issue in the way they would like to

Let's look at points 3 and 4 in more detail:

We need to be aware of the power dynamics of the supervisor/ supervisee relationship. The supervisee might want to go in a particular direction but if the supervisor suggests something or asks a leading question, it's possible the supervisee will follow the suggestions of the supervisor. This can mean that the supervisee doesn't get to explore the issue in the way they would like to.

In order to get a clear *focus*, we need to follow the process. In this part of the process, we can ask the person questions that are phrased in a way to help the supervisee gain clarity. We use words such as 'aspect' and 'walk away with' to facilitate the process of getting a clear *focus*. We take time to ask these questions *before* we start to interact with them about the specifics of the situation or issue.

For example, we might ask:

➡️ "In regards to this situation, what aspect of it would you like to focus on in the session today?"

➡️ "By the time we have finished the session today, what would you like to walk away with?"

Using the scenario about the person who felt they were treated unfairly at work, we have to be careful we don't assume we know what they want from the session. There are many different aspects that they may want to focus on, such as:

➡️ "I'd like to explore what I did wrong. Was it my fault that I didn't get that promotion?"

➡️ "I'm so angry at my boss, after all I have done, how could she do that to me? I can't seem to get past this anger I have... maybe we could look at that?"

➡️ "I would like to really focus on my relationship with my boss, we used to get on so well, but something seemed to change, and I'd like to reflect on our relationship."

➡️ "I have to make a decision what to do about it. Do I leave the organisation or stay? I'd like to discuss this."

➡️ "This is the best thing that has ever happened to me. I really didn't feel working in this organisation was a good fit for me and I'm thinking about leaving anyway."

⮕ "I would like to spend some time today getting a clear sense of the type of job that I could get that I would love."

What you may notice here is there are many ways that you can interact with a single issue that a person brings to supervision. Allowing the time to really check with the person what they are wanting is so important or we can find ourselves leading the session and focusing on what we 'think' the person wants.

The person may not be clear themselves, so slowing it down and asking them what they want to *focus* on helps them to consider this and get clarity. Otherwise, you can in effect waste the session looking at an aspect that is not what's needed by the supervisee but just follows your agenda as a supervisor.

Without a clear *focus* from the supervisee, it can be difficult to enter the reflective space (which is in the next element: *Reflect*). Be careful that the *focus* has not been chosen by you (the supervisor) as what *you* choose might not be what the *supervisee* really wants.

In summary, if you <u>don't</u> have a clear *focus* then:

⮕ it's not clear what the supervisee wants

⮕ you may not get into the reflective space at all

⮕ you can end up asking lots of questions, which can seem like an interrogation

⮕ it results in lots of general conversation

⮕ you may both get caught in the story, and may not enter the process of supervision

⮕ no real supervision 'work' happens

⮕ the session can stall leaving you thinking:

"What do we do now??"

In summary, if you <u>do</u> have a clear *focus* then:

➡ you identify what the supervisee specifically wants from the supervision session

➡ you know what aspect of their story (experience) they want to *focus* on today

➡ you both intentionally enter the reflective space knowing the *focus*

➡ a reflective supervision tool can be utilised (one that is appropriate for the *focus*)

➡ an 'aha' moment may happen as the supervisee is engaged in the process of supervision

➡ the supervisee can 'see things differently' specifically around the *focus* area

➡ the 'work' and 'process' of supervision happens

Once there is a clear contract and clear *focus* then it's time to move to the next element: *Reflect* (to gain perspective and greater clarity).

Reflect

I'm not naturally a reflective person. I like to move quickly to action. But I have learnt over time the importance of *reflection* and the value of stopping, walking around something to look at it from a different angle and gaining new perspectives.

In the reflective space, you are <u>not</u> trying to fix the situation, give advice or find solutions. Instead, in this important space, you are giving the supervisee the opportunity to *reflect* on the situation.

By having the chance to reflect, the supervisee can look at things through a different lens or from another angle. *Reflection* allows the supervisee to notice things they may not have noticed before; to look at the situation without distractions and without someone else's opinion.

Preparing to enter the reflective space

I have found it helpful to think of the reflective space as a swimming pool. You and your supervisee are standing on the edge of the pool ready to jump in.

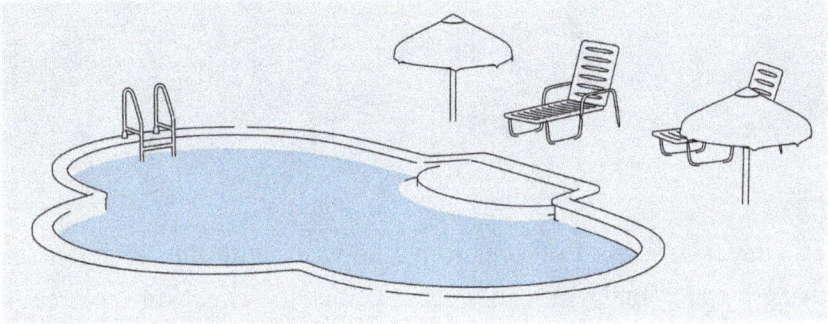

We could use the analogy of pool toys to represent the focus for the session. If we jump into the pool with lots of pool toys, we can become overwhelmed, as we don't know which one to focus on.

We just start looking at toys as they float past, such as a beach ball and then a noodle, and these items catch our attention. Then a blow-up flamingo touches us, and we are distracted by that pool toy.

If we have a clear focus, then we only take *one toy* into the pool. That makes it very clear and easy to know *what* we are going to do in the pool (the reflective space).

As a supervisor, part of your role is to work with the supervisee to create a space that you can enter together to *reflect* on the area of focus.

Using this analogy of a swimming pool to represent the reflective space in a supervision session, consider for a moment what it might be like to get in the pool:

▷ Is the temperature hot, cold or warm?
   (What is the atmosphere like in the supervision session?)

▷ Is the water calm, rough or choppy?
   (Are you providing a calm, peaceful supervision space?)

▷ Is the pool inviting or does it seem dangerous?
   (Is the supervision space inviting and does it feel safe?)

➡ Are you going to swim or float?
(Are you going to be able to stop and reflect or are you working too hard in the session?)

➡ What is it like for the supervisee to get in the swimming pool?
(Is your supervisee a person that is used to and comfortable to enter the reflective space?)

➡ What is it like for you to enter the swimming pool?
(Are you a person that is used to and comfortable to enter the reflective space?)

➡ Are you both going to jump or dive into the pool or are you going to use the steps?
(Are you jumping straight into the reflective space or going in slowly?)

Once you have <u>one clear focus</u> for the session and you feel you have prepared to enter the reflective space, then - you get into the pool together, taking *just one pool toy.*

So, you are in the pool together now with the pool toy: what do you do next? You decide together how you would like to *reflect* on this situation or issue around the aspect that you are going to focus on.

Let's say the supervisee wanted to focus on her relationship with her boss. She spoke of how they used to get on so well, but something seemed to change, and she said she would like to *reflect* on their relationship.

There are many ways to *reflect* on this: the main objective is to assist the supervisee to gain new perspectives and greater clarity as to what might be going on.

➪ You can put the issue or situation in the middle and walk around it and look at it from different angles and see if there is something that the person hasn't seen before

➪ You can use one of the reflective models, tools or resources that you can find in this book (such as picture cards, drawing the situation and many more) which can assist the person to see the situation from new perspectives

Try and stay impartial when in the reflective space with them. If you can stay objective then that's when you are the most helpful to the supervisee. Try to not fall into collusion or end up defending a person or organisation or a particular viewpoint. If you take sides, you become part of the person's story and it's hard to then be someone who can take a step back and see the bigger picture.

Sometimes as the supervisor, we can find ourselves tempted to take our eyes off the supervisee and their toy and jump out and grab one of our own toys, such as:

➪ comparing the supervisee's situation or issue to a time when something similar happened to us

➪ saying we have an idea about the situation or issue

➪ putting forward a solution that might fix the problem

If you think you have something to offer, there is a possibility that your point may be helpful but at this stage, it's usually better to hold back until you are out of the reflective space (*the pool*).

In other words, while you are still in the reflective space: **wait!** Otherwise, your well-meaning comment might inadvertently **stop** the process of supervision from happening.

If you recognise that you are in the pool <u>without</u> a clear focus (*there's lots of pool toys floating around*), take some time to:

➪ check back in with the contract (*the topic*)

➪ pause for a moment to get clarity on the focus (*choose one specific pool toy and remove any others*)

➪ be with the supervisee in the reflective space – trust the process

The reflective space is part of the process of supervision, so if you manage to enter this space with a clear focus, and stay there long enough, you will be amazed at what happens.

You really can trust the supervision process to assist your supervisee to have their 'aha' moment: to see the situation with much more clarity and from a different perspective. Once this has happened, it's time to *get out of the pool* in order to leave the reflective space.

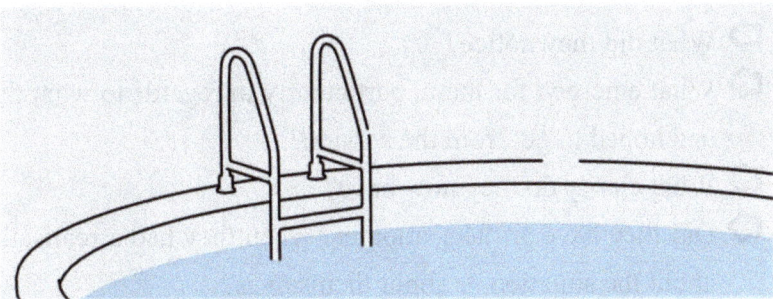

You don't want to end the session while you are still in the pool as the supervisee might be in a vulnerable or unstable position (*left in the pool alone, without your support*): you need to bring this step of the process to a conclusion.

You get out the pool <u>together</u>, dry off and then sit on the deck chairs to discuss what happened in the pool (the next element: *Summary*).

Summary

You are now both sitting out of the pool, by the water. You have moved to the next element: *Summary*. That is, you now ask the supervisee what it was like being in the pool…

➪ What did they notice?
➪ What emerged for them, particularly in regards to what they had hoped to get from the session?
➪ What clarity do they now have?
➪ Did they have an 'aha' moment when they had a realisation about the situation or about themselves?

So much of what happens in the reflective space is about *who we are* as well as *what we do*. It can be so powerful to gain a new insight.

During the summary, you may like to offer the supervisee a perspective that they have not yet considered, especially if they are fairly new to their role or profession.

Once all these things have been considered, and we have discussed what they have discovered, it's time to move to the next element: *Action*.

Action

Now that your supervisee has this new insight, what does that mean for them going forward? Will they do anything differently now that they have spent this time in reflection?

The *action* step in the process is where the supervisee may want to discuss options with you. Remember to always look to empower your supervisee.

I sometimes ask the person what *action* they will take by enquiring:

"What will you do straight after the session today?"

The next step or *action* can be to do <u>further reflection</u>. A supervision session can be the start of reflection rather than the place where it's all resolved and tied up with a neat bow before they leave.

The *action* may be to put a plan in place or to have a conversation with someone. There may be some other *action* item. It's good to check with your supervisee by asking what action they are going to take as a result of the supervision session.

We then move to the next element: *Review*.

Review

This is where, in a way, you *step out* of the process of supervision in order to *review* the process. To do this, ask the supervisee how the session was for them today:

➪ What was it like to engage in the process?

➪ What really stood out for you?

➪ What are you taking with you from the session?

In addition to the more general questions, you may like to ask particular questions about the focus area that you had decided together to work on in the session, in order to find out if they received what they were hoping for.

In the *review* stage, you might agree to contract to 'relook' at something in the next session (if both supervisor and supervisee think it's needed).

In this final stage of the model, as you reach the end of the session, the supervisor would usually book in (or clarify details) about the next appointment. I find this to be a good practice because it helps to ensure that the booking for the next session is in place.

Timing in the Supervision Session

The supervisor and supervisee would generally decide on the length of time a session is going to last. When I'm in my supervisor role, I usually book sessions for one hour.

You may be interested to know how I spread my time as I follow the supervision process across the hour. I've written a guide on the next page for a supervision session with a supervisee who has seen me at least once before (NB: This is <u>not</u> the structure I would use for the first session with a new supervisee). Whilst I am flexible to make adjustments if needed, the timing would be roughly divided as follows:

➡ I would on average spend around 10 minutes reconnecting where I *listen* to them as they share (their story/*experience*)

➡ We would then spend around another 10 minutes on the session *contract* and the *focus* for the session

➡ The *reflection* would usually go for around 20 minutes

➡ We would stay in the *summary* and *action* for about 10 minutes

➡ I would usually allow around 10 minutes for the *review* which would include the time needed for booking the next appointment

This is a very general guide as sometimes I would spend a lot longer in one of the sections: it all depends on the person and the day.

I feel it's respectful to the supervisee to try to start and finish on time and it also models good boundaries.

A Word of Caution – Getting Stuck in the Listening Loop

The Perspective Supervision Process Model gives us a road map to follow so that we can be confident that we will get to the end of the session having achieved what we set out to do.

If we review the beginning steps of the model, we can clearly see that moving from the element: *listen* to the element: *contract* is a key step. This important step ensures that what is happening in the session **is supervision**.

Put another way, moving from *listen* to *contract* enables us to *enter* the process of supervision.

What happens if we don't make this important step?

If we don't progress from listening to contract, the session can end up with you just listening to the supervisee's story for the whole time. When this happens, as seen in the model below, we find ourselves 'stuck' in the top right-hand corner, in a **listening loop**.

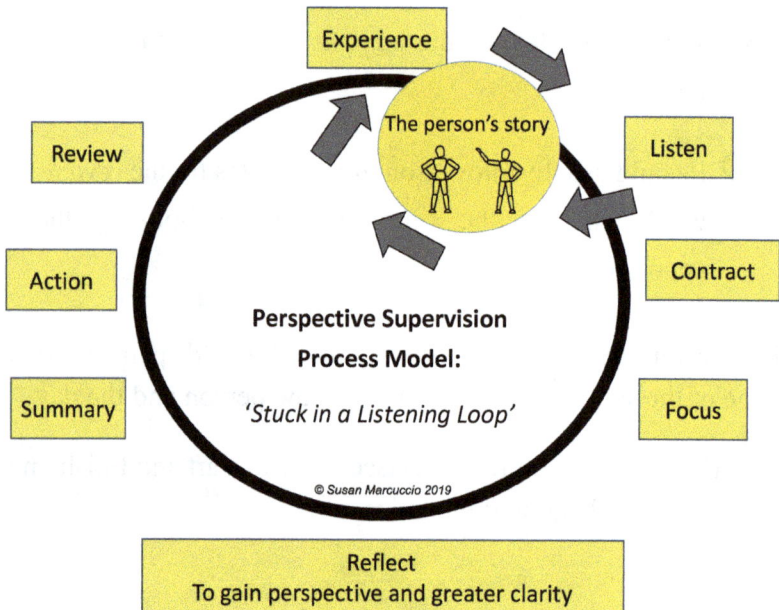

This has happened to me in a supervision session when I was in the role of supervisor – I got stuck in a **listening loop**. I remember it as a time when the person seemed like they really *wanted to talk* and share their story, so I decided to *just listen*.

While *listening* is a great thing to do in a chaplaincy role and in some other contexts, in supervision, we actually want to *enter* the process of supervision. This is one of the reasons why having a process model to follow is so helpful for supervisors. The steps of the process model keep us 'on track' to provide supervision by ensuring that we *really enter the process.*

Well, on this day, I <u>didn't</u> enter the process of supervision. I just stayed and listened and never went to the next step of the process: to *contract* for the session.

To recap, contracting is the element in the process where we discuss what the supervisee would like to 'work on' or 'work with' in the session. We decide together what we are going to do on that day in the supervision session. It doesn't just happen: we are very deliberate about it.

On this particular day, I <u>didn't</u> contract with my supervisee. I just decided to listen to her story. I listened well and thought to myself:

"This is what she must have wanted today so I guess it's fine that I just listened. It's about what *she wants*, not what *I want*."

How wrong I was! At the end of our time together, I asked her what she was going to take from the supervision session, and she said:

"Well... actually nothing."

I was a bit shocked.

"I feel like all you did was just listen to me," she went on to say, "and we didn't really get anywhere with it."

She was right!

I learnt a valuable lesson that day about entering or in this case *not entering* the process of supervision. So, make sure you progress past listening and *contract* for the session.

NEW PERSPECTIVES MODEL

Here we will introduce a new model called the 'New Perspectives Model' which has been designed to show the importance of first listening, then making the *timely progression* into the other elements in the 'Perspective Supervision Process Model'. This new model takes us even more slowly through the first elements of the process so we can be mindful to *not get stuck* in the 'listening loop'.

NEW PERSPECTIVES MODEL: DIAGRAM ONE

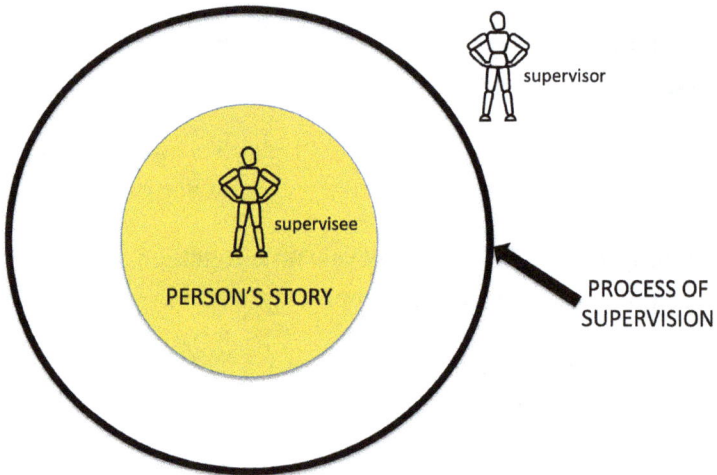

(Susan Marcuccio 2022)

IN DIAGRAM ONE, the supervisee arrives at their supervision session with a story to tell *(represented by the yellow circle)*. As the supervisor, we are looking to assist the supervisee to enter into the process of supervision.

NEW PERSPECTIVES MODEL: DIAGRAM TWO

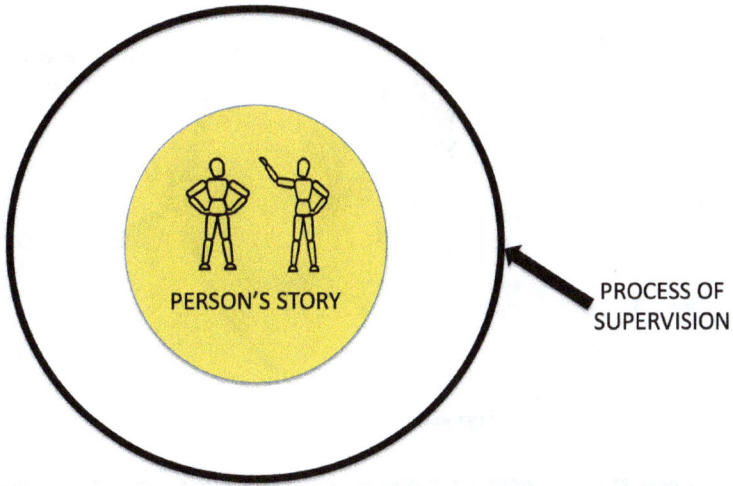

New Perspectives Model

PERSON'S STORY

PROCESS OF
SUPERVISION

(Susan Marcuccio 2022)

IN DIAGRAM TWO, we go into the space with the supervisee and hear their story. While we are in this space, we hear the story from the supervisee's perspective.

We want to be present in the moment with them, to listen to their story and show empathy. It's important to honour the person's story.

NEW PERSPECTIVES MODEL: DIAGRAM THREE

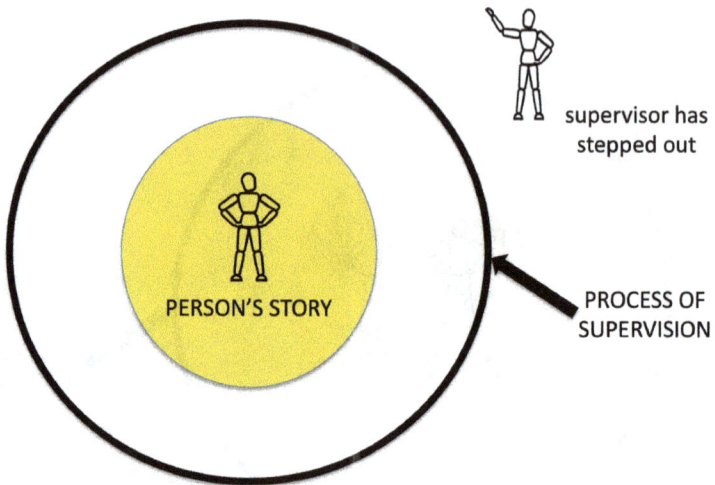

(Susan Marcuccio 2022)

IN DIAGRAM THREE, an important move happens:

The supervisor leads the way to the next element by *stepping out of the story.*

Moving through the Elements of the Process Model

As the supervisor, we go into the story (*listen*) and then step out again (in order to move to *contract*). Why is this necessary?

➡ If, as the supervisor, I am able to first go into the story with the supervisee and be present, listen and show empathy, then we make that important connection.

➡ By being *with* the supervisee in the story, we get to hear the story from their perspective.

➡ Then, as the supervisor, if I step out of the supervisee's story, I can see things more clearly, from a broader perspective.

While they may feel supported, which is important, staying with the supervisee in the story doesn't give them the opportunity to see more broadly.

Being Mindful of Not Getting Stuck in the Listening Loop

If we, as the supervisor, are *stuck in the listening loop*, getting the supervisee to step out of the story doesn't usually happen. Instead of progressing to the next elements in the process (*contract, focus, reflect*), we both end up staying in the story.

What are some of the reasons why, as supervisor, we might get stuck in the listening loop and fail to progress to *contract, focus and reflect?*

➡ We get so moved by the story that we get caught up in it

➡ We find it hard to stop listening to the story

➡ We don't want to interrupt them as they tell the story

It's important, as supervisor, to step out of the story. But it's not enough to just *tell* the supervisee what you can now see from your new position outside the story. That's because, while they are *still in the story*, the supervisee can *only see things* from **their perspective**.

New Perspectives Model

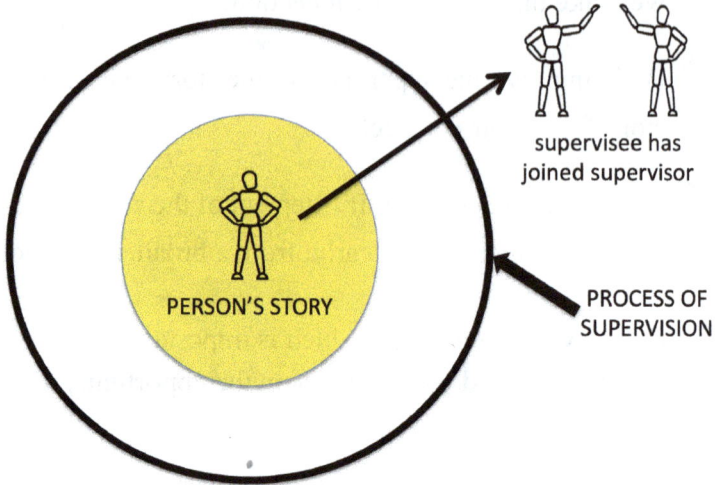

supervisee has
joined supervisor

PERSON'S STORY

PROCESS OF
SUPERVISION

(Susan Marcuccio 2022)

IN DIAGRAM FOUR, we see the supervisor inviting the supervisee to also step out of the story. This enables the supervisee to *enter* the process of supervision where they will see the situation more broadly and with greater clarity.

If the supervisee steps out of their story and engages in the process of supervision, they have the opportunity to:

➡ *contract* for the session
➡ choose the aspect they want to *focus* on
➡ *reflect* on the aspect from outside the story
➡ see the situation from *new perspectives*

The supervisee can then go on and complete the process of supervision by moving through the final elements of summary, action and review. This process really can be life changing!

Practicalities of Providing Supervision

Overall Contract

We have already covered contracting for each session, but we also need to look at the overall contract that you would establish with your supervisee. Some of this would happen before your first session and some would be discussed during the first session.

a) Where are we going to meet?

You need to consider where a suitable place is to meet. I have used a mixture of Zoom, Skype, my own office, a church room, a room at an allied health clinic, and I also go to an organisation's building or church building for the day and see their staff throughout the day.

If you use an office, it's a good idea to have a glass door or panel if possible so it's private for confidentiality reasons but people can still *see in,* providing safety for you and your supervisee.

It's important to find a location that works well for you and your supervisee. However, in my experience, there are difficulties meeting in some locations such as a coffee shop or similar as it may not be private enough and can be noisy and distracting.

b) How often are we going to meet?

I usually suggest meeting with a supervisee once a month for one hour but this is dependent on a number of factors such as whether the individual or organisation is paying for the session. The individual has more flexibility but may be limited by cost; the organisation usually has a particular amount of sessions per year that they will pay for.

Some people I see once every six weeks or two months, and some would be every three months. It is ideal to see people regularly as it is difficult to supervise people when you don't see them very often.

Irregular supervision tends to be more reactionary rather than preventative.

It is also a good idea to contract for a particular number of sessions and schedule in a review part way through. With my regular supervisees, we usually agree to meet for a certain number of sessions in a twelve-month period and do a review at the end of the year (as well as sometimes part way through the year).

To start with, you may like to contract together for four sessions and then discuss to see if you would both like to continue. This makes it very clear as to what you have both agreed to.

When possible, I always book in the next appointment at the end of the session as if you don't, people often forget to book in or they prioritise other people over themselves. It's a good habit to get into as it helps the person plan and make it a priority. I always send a text reminder the day before and usually email an invoice to the person within a week of the session.

c) What are they hoping to get from supervision?

In the very first session I have with someone, I usually spend the first 30 minutes on the overall contract which includes sharing the 'Three Ringed Model' and discussing the functions of supervision: support, best practice and learning (Leach & Paterson, 2015).

I ask them if there is anything from what I have just shared that really stands out that they are hoping to get from supervision, and we spend some time discussing this and may set some goals for what they'd like to get from supervision.

I usually ask the person to share how they ended up in the role they are in. This keeps the focus on work but gives them the opportunity to share what's important for them at that time. I also give them the opportunity for any questions they may have for me.

I use the second half of the first session to do a mini supervision session so they get a taste for what it's like to enter into the process of supervision. I find that if you don't do this, the person's first impression of supervision is 'about' supervision rather than 'doing' supervision, and there is a big difference.

I contract for the actual second half of the supervision session using the 'Perspective Supervision Process Model'.

I have included the above information as sometimes it can be helpful to hear what someone else does. I have developed my own style which works for me, and I imagine you either have or will 'also develop your own style'.

Supervision Container

While it is important to allow the supervisee to set the agenda for the session and to choose what they would like to share and focus on, we also have a duty of care for our supervisees. Occasionally, we have to override what they want to talk about.

I liken the combination of our duty of care and the obligations that we have to our supervisee as being a 'supervision container'.

Just as a container provides a defined space, we 'hold a space' for the supervisee and for the session. We adhere to obligations that also play a part in holding the session together. So, the 'supervision container' is like a protective barrier that holds the space around the supervision session.

Areas where we need to override the agenda for the session and may have to break confidentiality if we have concerns include:

➡ Duty of care issues

➡ Mandatory reporting

➡ Illegal activity

➡ Harm to self or others

➡ If the person is not fit for their role

➡ If we have a concern about a person's self-care

➡ Any other areas that we have contracted with the supervisee or their organisation

➡ Breach of code of ethics or code of conduct or similar

It is important to discuss this with your supervisee when you set up the overall contract with them. You may like to document and include relevant aspects in a written contract so it's really clear upfront.

It is indeed a privilege to enter into the process of supervision with someone. If you haven't had the opportunity to either provide supervision or engage in it yourself, can I encourage you to take the plunge and:

Trust the process of supervision!

CHAPTER FIVE

LOSS, GRIEF AND RESILIENCE

What has happened
It can't be true
No, I don't believe it
I feel like I am floating
Separated from my body
Stop the world

My heart has been ripped out
I can't breathe
I feel so strange
Can't find my words
The world is spinning
Somebody help me

I'm standing alone
Yet with many others
I am finally anchored
Yet, here we go again
Riding the wave of pain
Thrown up on the shore

When Grief Becomes Personal

"Go straight to Emergency!" These are the words every mother dreads to hear about their child. Quite ironic after years of working in emergency wards, supporting others...

After weeks of not knowing what was wrong with our 26-year-old son, the doctors had finally tried a different test and found 'something'. So, to emergency we went, and after many hours of waiting and further tests, we were told that our son had a tumour in his brain stem.

That was the moment that everything changed.

Our family all congregated at the hospital in shock and disbelief. He was admitted to hospital and his brain surgery was planned. As a hospital chaplain, I suddenly found myself on the other side. Not the one *coming alongside* a family, but now part of the family that *needed support*. To make things more complicated, I was the step mum.

The day of the surgery was difficult beyond belief. They told us that the surgery was very dangerous but that there was really no other option. Going into the brain stem area to try and remove the tumour was like trying to get 'sand out of jelly'. Saying goodbye to our son before he went into surgery was so hard - we really didn't know if we would see him again.

Sitting in the hospital cafe while he was in surgery, waiting for the call, was agonising. Finally, the good news came that he had survived the surgery and they had managed to get some of the tumour out without doing too much damage to the brain stem. What a relief.

The next bit of news was not so good. He was diagnosed with brain cancer, stage three anaplastic astrocytoma. We were told he would need to have radiotherapy and chemotherapy. The journey to fight this disease went into full swing.

His older brother was due to be married a few weeks after the surgery. Our son, who was sick, was the best man. I was so proud of our whole family, how everyone rallied around and supported each other. There were times of real pain and chaos as everyone coped with the situation the best they knew how.

After difficult discussions, it was decided to still go ahead with the wedding but to cancel all the preliminary celebrations prior to the wedding such as the buck's and hen's nights. No one really felt like celebrating.

Sadly, it didn't look like there was any hope of our son being able to attend the wedding and be best man as he was too sick and hooked up to different machines in hospital, so other arrangements were made.

The day before the wedding, he decided that he really wanted to be there, so we managed to get him a day pass out of the hospital and quickly arranged a suit for him to wear. He was so brave and stood proudly next to his older brother as his best man.

Even though he was unwell, he showed such strength of character – making the day about his brother, the groom and his bride. While a highly emotional day for all involved, it was a beautiful wedding and we all had a much-needed respite from the dark cloud that was looming over us all.

A few weeks before the diagnosis, I had just started at a new job, overseeing the chaplaincy training at a college. I was grateful for the wonderful support I received and after a few weeks off, I went back to work.

A very well-meaning person entered my office after my few weeks away and said to me:

"Why are you here? Your priorities are elsewhere."

What was intended as a supportive comment absolutely devastated me. I really learnt that day that we need to be so careful with our words: we never really know what's going on for someone.

While it was hard for me to *not be* at home, my husband had taken some time off work to do house renovations, so when our son got sick, it became the obvious choice for *him* to stay home as the carer and for *me* to go back to work to pay the bills. For some of the time, it became my daily routine to be at work all day and then at the hospital all evening.

We had such incredible support from our family and friends as well as our church family, who dropped off meals, did the gardening and helped with financial assistance. A particular memorable gesture was one Christmas morning:

Christmas is a big deal for me. I would say it's my favourite day of the year, having time with family, exchanging gifts, and sharing a meal. Well, this Christmas, our son was in hospital, so we decided to all meet at the hospital and exchange gifts in his room, as he couldn't come home and we didn't want him to miss out. We were just about to leave for the hospital when there was a knock at the door. A friend of ours from church was standing at the door with her young son. They were holding Christmas lunch for us, all packed up to take to the hospital.

Thinking of that act of kindness still makes me emotional. What a wonderful example for her son to do that for someone on Christmas morning. I will never forget it. You don't know what a difference it can make for someone to offer thoughtful kindness.

A couple of years later we were all sitting at the cafe at the hospital and were given the news that, despite the treatment holding the cancer at bay for a while, the tumour had started to grow again and this time - *there was nothing they could do*. While we were aware that this could eventually be the reality, nothing really prepares you for this news.

Our son had become engaged and he and his fiancé had planned to have their wedding in around six months' time. The doctors advised that it would need to happen much quicker than that.

So, with death looming and not really knowing what to do to process this tragic news, we all went into full steam planning of a wedding. It was what they wanted so - it became the focus.

Not long after that we were at their wedding. By this time, our son could no longer walk and was confined to a wheelchair. He also had difficulty talking. He did however manage to say his vows and at the reception, managed to stand up for a short while to do the bridal waltz. There was not a dry eye in the house... such an emotional moment.

They had a few months living together as a married couple, but before long, he got so sick, he was unable to remain out of hospital. It was extremely hard seeing him unable to walk or talk and eventually, unable to swallow. The day we finally had to take him to hospital, we found ourselves back in emergency where it had all started.

They asked us the question on admission:

"Do you want *do not resuscitate* on his file?"

I'll never forget that moment, the reality of the situation hit me. We answered with a very strong: **"No**, we don't want you to put that on his file - if anything happens, we want him to be resuscitated!"

After a week in hospital, it was decided that he would come home *once he was stabilised*, and we would care for him for what looked likely to be his final few months.

While he was in hospital, there was a huge storm across NSW which caused trees to come down and lots of flooding. The electricity went off at our home and across the local area, with even the hospital resorting to back up electricity sources. The mobile phone service was also affected with no signal much of the time.

It was at this stage that it started to become clear that he may not be able to come home. We were at the hospital *all day* and *all night*, only returning home late at night to sleep. His wife stayed with him practically the whole time.

After four days with no power, limited phone signal and almost our whole garden and part of our road flooded, we headed into the hospital. I remember waking up that morning and having a sense that *this was the day.*

When we arrived at the hospital, we found our daughter in law and his mum in the family waiting area in the ward as he was having a procedure to make him more comfortable. Just after we arrived, a nurse came in and said that they couldn't wake him up.

We all rushed to his bedside, and they informed us it was unlikely that he would wake up again. The rest of the family rushed to get to the hospital, driving through roads with trees down and debris everywhere. The next few hours, we all sat with him until he breathed his last breath.

That afternoon, we all went back to our place. We still didn't have power so as night fell, we all sat on our balcony with portable lights hooked up somehow. Looking back, we could have gone to someone else's place that had power but we all just wanted to be there at our place where he and his wife also lived.

The next few days were a blur of planning a funeral and trying to deal with the reality that he was gone. A few days later, the storm had subsided but there was a freak hailstorm. We were all still sitting on the balcony at our place and the hail was so big and so loud I remember thinking to myself: *"It's the end of the world..."*

It seemed like the world had gone mad - nothing was the same any more... and it really wasn't the same.

Our lives had been changed forever.

What I Have Learnt About Loss and Grief

I have learnt so much about loss and grief over the past few years. I had taught on this subject for many years prior to my son's illness and I knew the theory well. Theory certainly helps with understanding what's happening, but nothing can prepare you for when you *actually experience it.*

I have had some difficult losses over my life, but this was different. It's hard to explain what grief feels like. For me, some days felt like there was an elephant sitting on my chest, and I could hardly breathe. Other days, it was so hard to accept that everyone seemed to still be living their lives, almost as though nothing had happened.

In those early months, I sometimes wanted to scream out:

"Don't you know what has happened? STOP!"

But people *do still keep living* because they have to, to survive.

I have noticed that everyone grieves so differently. Some people like to have reminders of the person everywhere as it helps keep them connected; others can't bear to see anything that reminds them of the person, as it's too painful. We have to be so careful not to judge others, as they are processing the grief the *best way they know how*.

I have created a model which I have called the 'Two Spaces Grief Processing Model'. My model was inspired by the Dual Processing Model of Coping with Bereavement (Stroebe & Schut, 2010).

Using this 'two spaces' model is one of the best ways I have found to help people get a sense of what's happening to them and the people around them when they experience a loss and are grieving.

The model can be used by supervisors, chaplains and mentors in their supportive roles. Equally, the model can be used by anyone who finds themselves in a situation where there is loss and grief.

As you read the next section, you might find yourself relating to the experience of grief, due to a loss in your own life or in those around you such as family members, friends or colleagues. Take your time, *if you need to*, as you read about loss and grief and the 'two spaces' model. Pause a moment, reach out to someone or come back to this section for a second look, when the timing is right for you.

TWO SPACES GRIEF PROCESSING MODEL

The Grief Space

This model firstly talks about the grief space: this is where people go to grieve, to allow themselves to feel the feelings, to cry or reflect, to look at photographs, remember, whatever they need to do to process the grief.

We are designed to grieve when we experience a loss, so this is a vital part of the process, to feel the pain and to allow ourselves time and space to do this.

⇔ Two Spaces Grief Processing Model

Grief Space   New Normal

(Susan Marcuccio 2017)

Some people go into the grief space easily, others find it really hard. Some are too scared to enter this space as they are worried they won't ever come out.

Sometimes people do get 'stuck' in the grief space: they can't get out of bed; they can't function. This may be very normal but eventually, the person may need to see a professional grief counsellor if they are stuck for a prolonged period.

The New Normal

On the right-hand side of the model is the space that I call the 'new normal'. This is where the person is able to function despite the loss they have experienced. It is the 'new normal' as things can never truly be the same again after a significant loss.

In the new normal, the person is usually able to go back to work, to care for others, to function in the various roles they have. Some people are much more comfortable with this 'new normal' space as they try and avoid the pain of the grief space.

Caregivers tend to be wired to care for others *first* and worry about themselves *later* which can be very helpful in the moment but can also trap people in this 'new normal' space. If they don't spend any time in the grief space, then their body can eventually throw them in there or it can turn into complex grief, and they may need to be referred to a grief counsellor.

The Healthy Way to Grieve

If the person is able to go between the two spaces, then this is the healthy way to grieve: to spend *some time* in the grief space and *some time* in the new normal. As life goes on, over weeks, months and years, people tend to spend *more time* in the new normal and *less time* in the grief space.

On anniversaries or special occasions, people may spend more time in the grief space as the feelings can be as intense as when they first experienced the loss.

A loss may not just be the loss of a loved one, it is really the loss of anything that you have a significant emotional investment in.

It is helpful to realise that these two different spaces exist and that those around you may be in a *different space* to you:

⇨ If you are in the grief space and someone else is in the new normal, then it can feel as though the other person *doesn't care*

⇨ If you are in the new normal and you see a person in the grief space, you may feel annoyed that they get to *stop and grieve* while you have to *keep going* and be responsible

If you are aware that the healthy way to grieve is for people to go between the two spaces, it can help you to understand that the other person is just in the space they need to be in *at that moment.*

I have used this Two Spaces Grief Processing Model so many times: I have drawn it on a napkin in a café, shared it over the phone, and used it in supervision, mentoring, chaplaincy and teaching sessions. I have found that it can be very helpful for people to have a better understanding of what's happening for them as it helps to normalise the process and also helps them to be more patient with others.

Reflecting on Personal Loss and Grief

Reading about loss and grief can sometimes bring up memories from the past or even make you think about recent or current events. If you find that this is happening for you now, you might like to pause for a moment: you could even ask yourself the question:

"Which space am I more comfortable in at this point in my life: the *grief space* or the *new normal*?"

When you have had a loss in the past, can you now reflect and perhaps see a pattern? Did you go between the two spaces: the grief space and your new normal?

As you think back, you may come to realise that you were 'stuck' in one space or the other for a period of time…

Unprocessed Grief

You may like to spend a moment now just considering if there is any *unprocessed grief* in your life… If there is, you could consider making a conscious decision to visit the 'grief space'.

If you would like to go into the grief space - what would it take for you to feel comfortable or ready to go? Would you like someone to be with you as you prepare to venture in there? A chaplain, mentor or supervisor could be someone that could assist you. Or, you may prefer someone known to you: a trusted friend, your doctor or a counsellor. You could reach out for support or you may feel able to go into the grief space *on your own*. Whatever you choose, know that moving between the grief space and the new normal is healthy and:

It's okay!

People process grief in many different ways: some journal, some talk it out and verbally process, some like to be alone and maybe walk on the beach, for others it's exercise, or painting, or just sitting somewhere quietly. It is very individual: you need to find what's *right for you*.

Words of Hope and Comfort for the Broken Hearted

For some people when they experience a loss, they are so overcome with emotion that they feel like their heart is smashed into pieces and will never recover.

> *I have learnt that when your heart breaks, it can actually* <u>*break open,*</u> *giving you a greater capacity to love, have compassion and sit with people in their pain...*

> ***ALSO***

> *If your heart breaks into pieces... it can be put back together, it will never be the same, **but** it can be made into something beautiful...*

Building Resilience

I have been asked to share a number of times on how I personally build resilience. Although people think of resilience as the ability to bounce back, I like to think of it as *bouncing forward*. I have discovered the ways that help me and would like to share them with you now:

Steps for Building Resilience:

⇨ Preparation
⇨ Process
⇨ Purpose
⇨ People
⇨ Perspective

Preparation

This is about being <u>prepared</u>: doing everything you can to be living holistically healthy. It's about examining your heart to see if you are holding any grudges, struggling to forgive someone or if there is any bitterness or offence in your heart. If you allow these things to penetrate your heart and pierce it, they can fester and it all becomes very unhealthy.

So, get prepared and start from a place of holistic health. It will give you the best chance of surviving things that come your way and still being able to bounce forward.

Process

The next step is to <u>process</u> any areas that you have 'stashed away' and not dealt with. It could be as simple as talking it through, writing it down or just reflecting on a situation and then letting it go. This may be something you can do yourself, or with a trusted friend, chaplain, mentor, or supervisor. If you feel stuck, then you may need to see a counsellor or a psychologist.

If you process any back log and then regularly see a supervisor, you will be taking healthy steps to ensure that you don't have a build-up of *unprocessed* emotions or situations that can stop you from being able to bounce forward.

Purpose

Knowing your <u>purpose</u> really gives you an anchor to hold on to when tough times come. When you have found your purpose in life, it will keep you afloat, even when you face difficult or devastating situations. It's like a lifeline that you can hold onto: even though you may feel like you are in a fog, you can hang on to the lifeline and it will help you to keep moving forward and not drift away.

Knowing your purpose is one of the reasons to connect with your calling as it sets you up well to be able to bounce forward and have resilience. Some people actually find their calling *during or after* a tragedy - they are compelled to *do something* and end up finding their purpose as they go through the experience.

People

Having the right <u>people</u> in your life before a crisis hits is one of the keys to resilience. Once a difficult situation comes, it's often too late to build these relationships as it's the last thing you feel like doing or have time for. If you have these strategic people in place as a support, then you can access the relationships you need when you find yourself in a hard place.

Think about who is in your circle: do you have a supervisor, mentor, life coach, a number of close friends? Take time to build and nurture your network of people who assist you to connect with your spirituality, your faith and that which gives you strength.

Perspective

Of course, having a new <u>perspective</u> is another key to resilience. Sometimes we are so caught up in a situation that we can only see one aspect. Being able to sit back and broaden our view gives us a much better picture of what is happening. This can make a huge difference.

Putting the situation in perspective means we can move to rational thought, rather than getting caught up in our emotions.

If you are a person of faith, then looking at an eternal perspective can help to resolve the dissonance (inconsistencies of thought) you may be experiencing when you have conflicting information that is challenging your beliefs. It can also give you hope for the future.

Authentic Emotional Resilience

For me personally, my faith in Jesus has had a huge impact on my ability to bounce forward and be emotionally resilient. I have been deeply encouraged by the way Jesus responded when Lazarus died (as told in the Biblical story in John 11). When Jesus saw Mary weeping and the other people wailing over the death of Lazarus, he became angry and deeply troubled and then, Jesus wept…

Jesus allowed the full force of the emotion to hit him – it's a great example of *authentic emotional resilience*. He felt the pain. He allowed himself to feel it and process it but didn't just stay there: He got up and did what he was called to do. I am so encouraged by this. It inspires me to allow myself to feel the emotions but then to get back up and live my calling.

Authentic emotional resilience isn't about denying that the circumstances have happened or about ignoring the feelings you have. It's about getting back up despite the circumstances and despite the overwhelming emotions you may feel.

You may also have found ways to process your own emotions and to stay resilient.

BUILDING RESILIENCE TOOL

I have developed the 'Building Resilience Tool' to assist people to build resilience. Use the information on the previous three pages (preparation, process, purpose, people and perspective) to complete the chart below. Fill in what you need to do to *build resilience*. The chart can also be used as a checklist – once you have set yourself some goals, come back to the list to see what areas still need work.

Steps to follow	Fill in what you need to do to BUILD RESILIENCE
Preparation	
Process	
Purpose	
People	
Perspective	

Going the Distance

Imagine your life is like running in a marathon and you are in the 'race of life'. You are wanting to get to the end of the race without dropping out or having to give up because something 'takes you out'.

I have discovered that what happens *to you* and *around you* can't actually take you out of the race. Circumstances can't take you out - only *you can*. What I mean by that is - it's what happens to you *internally* that can take you out and stop you going the distance.

You need resilience to keep moving forward. Building resilience is about building *internal fortitude*.

Imagine you are walking (or maybe you're running) along the journey of life from the start of your life to the finish. The arrows represent the external circumstances that can come against you and try and take you out of the race. If you're taken out, you won't get to live your best life.

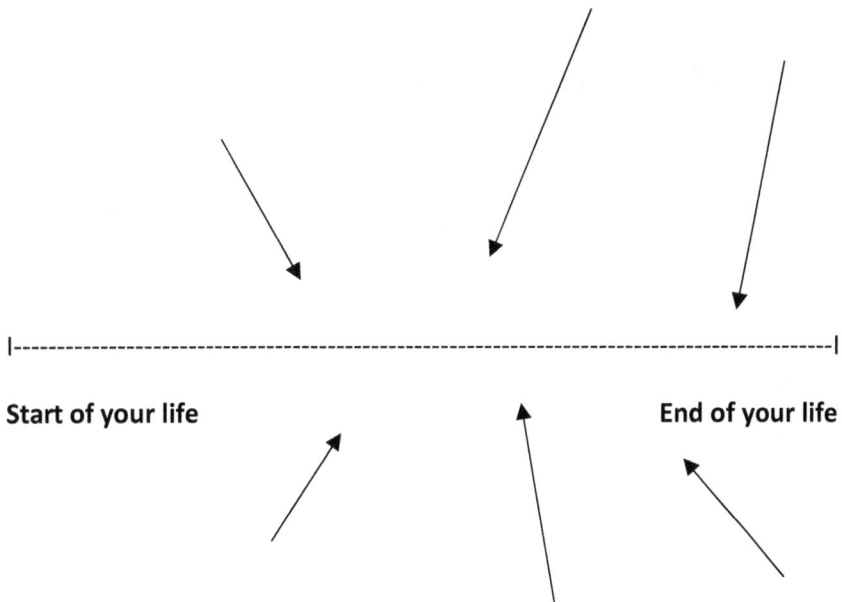

Start of your life   **End of your life**

We don't have control over external circumstances, but we do have control over our internal responses.

I have developed a checklist of areas that we need to monitor to ensure that we do all we can to go the distance and not drop out of the race. If we don't give time and energy to these areas, we can find ourselves giving up on:

⇨ our dreams
⇨ our calling
⇨ our purpose

If we give up on these fundamental parts of ourselves, we can end up living a life that is less than all we hoped for.

If you don't look after yourself and the fundamental areas of your life, everything else can fail.

You may feel you are doing well, and don't need to monitor or 'check' any areas in your life. If this sounds like you, then that's great! However, before you decide to skip over the list, here are some possible beliefs you may have around reflecting on your own self-care.

Some of these beliefs may already be known to you while others may be reflective of what's going on for you internally.

Possible beliefs about your own self-care, and your personal and professional growth and development:

⇨ I don't have any losses – *I don't need to grieve*
⇨ I haven't been offended by anyone – *my heart is fine*

➡ I'm not stressed or burnt out – *there's just a lot going on*

➡ I'm really healthy: physically, emotionally, spiritually, cognitively – *I don't need any support or to change anything*

➡ I know all I need to know – *I don't need to grow and develop*

➡ I'm living authentically – *I can be truly myself*

➡ I'm living the life I imagined – *I don't need to change*

➡ I know my purpose – *I'm connected to my calling*

➡ I'm great with people – *I don't need to improve this*

➡ I'm happy with my beliefs - *I'm connected to what gives my life meaning*

If all the statements above are true, then wow! Well done!

Room for Improvement

We can deceive ourselves though. Be brave and honest with yourself, there may be room for improvement in these areas. I suspect there is room for us all to improve our self-care and build our internal fortitude and resilience.

Let's look at the list again in the table on the next page.

I'm truly of the belief that neglecting any of the areas listed can be the very thing that can 'take you out of the race'.

I encourage you to work on the internal areas of your life that you **can do something about**. This will enable you to thrive in your profession and ultimately, in your life.

You might like to think of the list as being something to follow to ensure that you can 'go the distance':

CHECKLIST FOR 'GOING THE DISTANCE'

Acknowledge your losses – *process your grief*
Deal with offences/being offended – *guard your heart*
Operate in your sweet spot – *just the right amount of stress (don't burn out)*
Stay holistically healthy – *physically, emotionally, spiritually, cognitively*
Pursue personal growth/development – *be who you need to be at each point*
Be authentic – *be who you really are and know what you believe*
Be strategic and intentional – *plan your life*
Know your purpose – *stay true to your calling*
Nurture key relationships – *know how to interact with people*
Know what you believe – *connect with what gives your life meaning*

For supervisors and mentors, this is a list you can use in a supervision or mentoring session as a checklist for people to see what is going on for them internally and whether there are areas they would like to work on. It could also assist with developing goals to work on together in supervision or mentoring.

CHAPTER SIX

TO CARE AND BE CARED FOR

Always thinking of others
Going the extra mile
Living kindness
Pouring out care
Moved with compassion
Giving without hesitation

Acknowledge them
Return the kindness
Put them first
Allow precious time
For rest and relaxation
Filling of the tanks

To give and receive
Care and be cared for
Life flowing through
Filled to overflow
Give out of abundance
Care for each and everyone

Walking Alongside

As I learnt the various supervision models and began to see the importance of helping people to engage in the process of supervision, I discovered something important. While the steps and structure of a supervision session are <u>key</u> to the process working, there's a danger of the delivery becoming too 'methodical' and 'mechanical'. When this happens, the supervisor may miss the fact that there is an *actual person* sitting across from them (in the room or on screen).

I had a supervisee who I had been meeting with for a few years. It had taken some time for us to work well together as she was very guarded and seemed a bit reluctant to bring cases and ethical issues that she was struggling with.

Over time, I seemed to gain her trust and she started to really open up about her struggles. This meant that we developed a wonderful working relationship.

This particular supervisee had reached retirement age and was finishing up in her role. I still recall our final supervision session. We reflected on the supervision journey that we had walked together, and she was able to share what a difference it had made for her to have this place to come to share what was going on for her. I was also able to share what a privilege it had been for me to walk this journey with her.

After she left that last session, I noticed how sad I was at the loss of the relationship. It really hit me that I would no longer know what was happening in her life or how she was doing.

Sometime later, I was walking in my local area down a tree lined road that I frequent often. I began reflecting on our last session together and the supervisory relationship that we had.

It then came to me: an image of her walking down the road. I saw her on her *journey through her life* and me getting on the road alongside and walking with her for a season.

During the time that I walked on the road with her, I was championing her on. I was there to listen, to stay with her as she cried and laughed, to be a place where she could be herself and be free of others' expectations and judgements.

I was there to talk about what gave her life meaning, her fears, and her struggles, the heartache as she shared the tragic losses in her life and the many challenges of working with people in desperate situations.

It was an honour to see the transformation in her life as she brought specific situations and cases to supervision. As we reflected on them together, she was able to gain insight and awareness of her own unique worldview and how that influenced how she saw and experienced the situations she found herself in.

By stopping and reflecting, she was able to see things from different perspectives and things became clearer. The incredible personal and professional growth that she experienced, by making the decision to trust someone to walk with her, was astonishing.

I realised that for us as supervisors, we step onto the road with people and walk with them for a season. Then, we step off the road, believing that *someone else* will walk with them for the next season.

That really helped me to let the person go, knowing that I had played my part in that person's journey. It also highlighted to me what people really want. We can be the best supervisor, have lots of skills and be able to expertly help people to enter into the process of supervision. However, what people really want is...

Authentic Genuine Relationships

If we look at this discovery in the context of supervision, then what people are really looking for is someone who is *genuinely interested* in them. Someone who will listen, really listen: not thinking about the next thing they will say but staying fully present in the moment with them.

Someone to show respect and empathy, to attempt to understand what it is really like to be in their situation. Someone to feel the feelings they have, and to be faced with reflecting on the situation they are experiencing.

The *authentic, genuine relationship* means so much more than the skills or qualifications that you bring or how smart you are or even how equipped you think you are to 'fix' things for them.

We do need to have structure in the session and clear boundaries in the relationship; we also need to hone our skills, knowledge and experience as a supervisor. But if we have <u>all that</u> and *no connection* with the supervisee, our time together will be more like a transaction than a meaningful encounter.

I'm so thankful that I gained such valuable insight as I pondered on the end of my time with this supervisee. It has really helped me to remember how important the relationship is between supervisor and supervisee and how much of a privilege it is to journey alongside someone for a season.

"Walking Down the Road"

We walk with people through different seasons in their life.
As supervisors, we don't try and get them
onto a different road; we help give them courage
to find their own path to walk along.
We may stop with them for a while, as they rest and reflect.
The privilege is to be invited to walk with them
for part of their journey...
and then, let them go
and trust that others will walk with them
the rest of the way...

The CARE Model

I wanted to share with others the revelation I had about journeying alongside people, so I developed 'The CARE Model'. This model provides practical steps to make sure that we remember the importance of the supervisory relationship. It can also be used in other contexts to highlight the importance of the working and supportive relationships you may have.

The CARE Model is comprised of four parts:

Connection, Awareness, Response and Empower

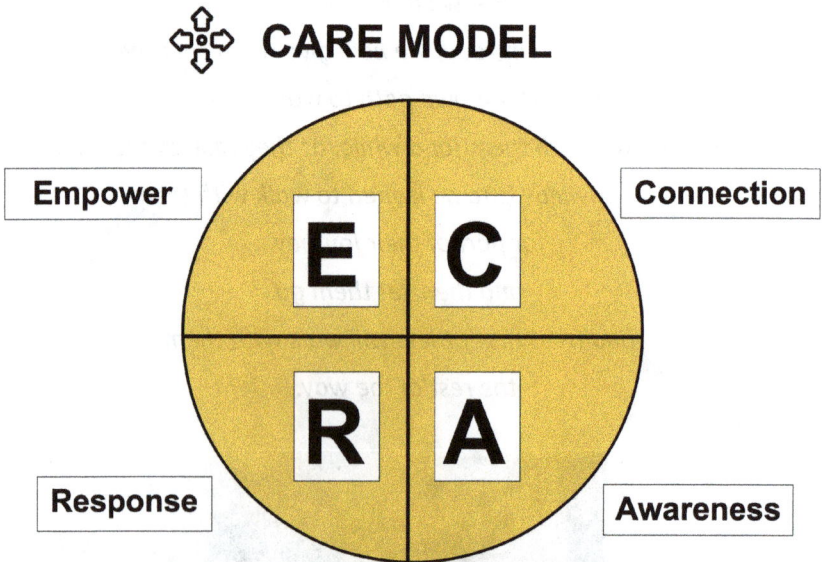

© Susan Marcuccio 2019

THE CARE MODEL

The CARE Model can be used by anyone as a way of providing care for someone. It can be a guide to provide support, firstly making a connection, then having awareness, then deciding how to respond and empower the person you are with.

The CARE Model can be a useful tool for chaplains as it provides a simple model to follow.

Supervisors and mentors can use the CARE Model as a process model, working their way through the different stages. Each stage builds on the next.

You start with *Connection* then move to *Awareness*, ensuring that you keep the *Connection*.

Then, keeping both *Connection* and *Awareness*, you move to *Response* and *Empower*.

The CARE Model can also be used by supervisors as a reflective tool to reflect on a supervision session and to see the session through this 'CARE' lens to gain new perspectives.

Supervisors can use this as a simple process model when they feel like they may be technically following the process of supervision but lacking connection with their supervisee.

Using the CARE Model

Connection

We start with connecting with the person, mindful of the role that we are in as a chaplain, mentor, supervisor or another role and keeping appropriate boundaries. Finding a way to connect is crucial.

⇔⬥ CARE MODEL

Connection.

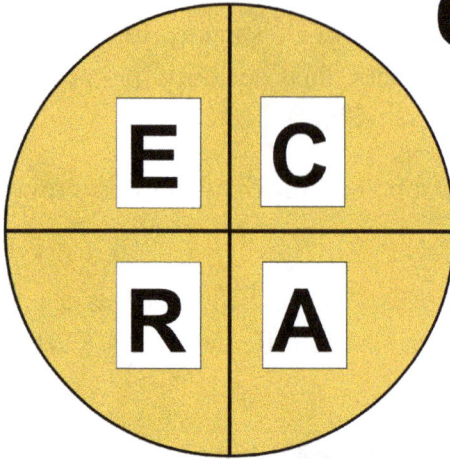

- Safe brave space
- Build rapport
- Fully present
- Clear role/s
- Listen
- Empathy
- Compassion
- Communication
- Non-judgemental
- Validate feelings
- Boundaries

© Susan Marcuccio 2019

I remember visiting a lady in my role as a chaplain. I asked her if she wanted a visit on this day. She looked at me and my badge, then said:

"No, thank you. I don't need a chaplain."

I had a choice to make. I could either just leave or make one more effort to make a connection.

I noticed some knitting on the table near her bed. So, I said to her:

"No problem. I'm just wondering though, before I leave, I just noticed that beautiful knitting you are doing. I would love to have a look at it if you don't mind."

Her face lit up.

"Yes, I would love to show you," she replied.

I went in and she showed me what she was working on and told me all about her grandchild that she was making the blanket for.

After spending quite some time with her at her request, we had a wonderful visit. She was able to share about some of the challenges she was facing and how much she appreciated my time.

What a difference it made by having a *connection* with her. She invited me to call in anytime I was passing. I could have just walked away and sometimes that is the right thing to do, but in this case, I just needed to make that important *connection*.

Once you have that *connection*, you keep it by:

- ⇨ spending time listening
- ⇨ being fully present
- ⇨ having empathy
- ⇨ showing compassion
- ⇨ creating a space for reflection, with no agenda or judgement
- ⇨ validating the person's feelings
- ⇨ letting the person know you are with them, they are not alone

Take the time to notice where the *connection* point is. There will be signs that you have connected, that the person trusts you and that they have confidence that your care for them is *genuine*.

In the context of supervision, I have found over and over again, how important *connection* is. What people really want is someone they can trust, someone who genuinely cares, so they can share freely and not feel judged. What a privilege it is to be in this space with someone. I just love it!

How often do we get the opportunity for someone to sit and focus just on us? That is such a major part of what supervision is, having someone to sit with you and just connect. Someone to listen and be fully present. When is the last time someone sat and listened to you and had that real *connection*? It's good to reflect on that, and if it's been sometime, then maybe you would benefit from having supervision yourself or finding a supervisor that you can connect with.

For supervisors, entering into the process of supervision is important, but if we don't have a *connection* with someone then it can just become like 'going through the motions'. The person won't let their guard down and there is not much chance of it being a meaningful encounter for them or for you.

If you are finding that you come away from a supervision session feeling like something is missing, then maybe work on your *connection* with the person.

Awareness

Awareness is another important part of caring for people. This goes hand in hand with connection. You really need to have *awareness* and connection working together.

To truly know if we have made a connection, we need to have *awareness* of what is happening for the other person and what is happening for you.

When you are truly present in the moment, and you have a connection with someone, you notice things that you may not have noticed before. You become more aware of how the person is responding to what you say and what you do.

You can wonder: what is it like for them to be here with me now? How are they feeling? What are they not saying? It is reading the cues of the person and being mindful of what's going on for them.

⬦ CARE MODEL

AWARENESS.

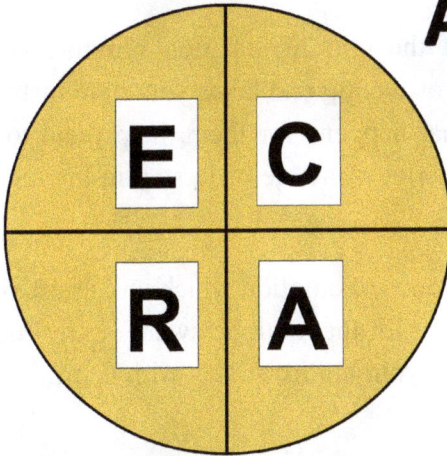

- What's happening:
  - ❖ Physically
  - ❖ Emotionally
  - ❖ Cognitively
  - ❖ Spiritually
- What's really going on?
- How are they feeling?
- What's not being said?
- Loss and grief
- Duty of care issues
- Triggers
- Transference

© Susan Marcuccio 2019

The person you are with may have recently had a loss that they are grieving, or aspects of their spirituality may have been challenged. We need to keep aware of any duty of care issues that they may be experiencing or carrying: something they may want to talk about.

Make sure there is enough space in your time together for them to tell you anything that they really want to say. Sometimes we try and fill in all the spaces and give no time for a pause in the conversation and the person can feel that you don't want to hear what they have to say.

In the context of supervision, be aware of that sacred space between you and them where you have connected. As the supervisor, knowing how you are feeling and how the encounter is impacting you and your ability to stay present is so important.

Ask yourself whether you can 'hold the space' for them and realise when you are triggered into your own thoughts and emotions. Either you or the person you are caring for may be experiencing a trigger.

Being 'triggered' is when the current situation reminds you of another situation or person or feeling and takes you there instead of being in the moment. If that happens for them, help them to stay grounded. If it happens for you, be aware of it, stay in the moment and process it later.

There may be some transference of emotion which will assist you to get a sense of what's going on for them but be aware of any counter transference that may impact your ability to stay with them.

Response

The next step is to consider your *response* to the person. Being able to respond while keeping the connection and awareness is really important. Being aware of what are they needing and wanting from you or if it is in the context of supervision, what they are wanting from the supervision session.

Know what you can do within the boundaries of your role. Respond in a way that the person or supervisee feels supported and cared for. That may simply be to hold the space for them and allow them to feel what they feel, process the emotion, and have the courage to keep going.

In the context of supervision, it's all about keeping the connection, being aware of what is happening and knowing what the supervisee is wanting to get from the session. This could be where you respond by offering a time of reflection where they can consider new perspectives regarding the situation.

✥ CARE MODEL

RESPONSE.

- What do they need?
- How can you help?
- What can you do?
- What must you do?
- Resources
- Referrals
- Reporting
- Providing care
- Providing support

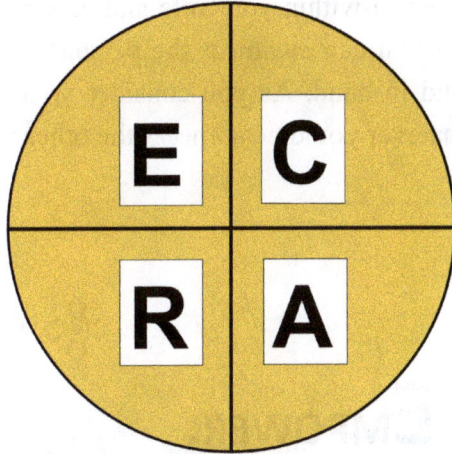

© Susan Marcuccio 2019

Remember the importance of the supervisory relationship: keeping the connection strong is key to the person feeling supported and cared for.

If they are needing something that you are unable to offer (as it's outside your role or capabilities), you may need to respond by providing resources or options for a referral to someone who can assist the person.

If there is a duty of care issue, then you may need to follow your organisation's policies and procedures around reporting and any other responsibilities.

Empower

Whilst keeping the connection and being aware of the appropriate response within your role and capability, the next step is to ensure that you can *empower* the person. Response and empowerment go hand in hand. As you consider your response, try and ensure that whatever you do *empowers* the other person.

⇱⇡⇲ **CARE MODEL**

Empower.

- Healthy boundaries
- Self esteem
- Not trying to fix
- Not your solutions
- Their options
- Their solutions
- Their decisions
- Ongoing support
- Follow up

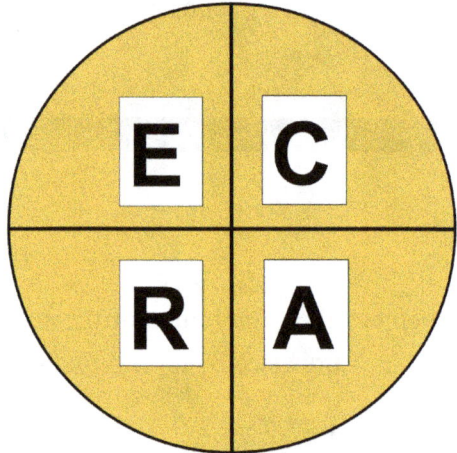

E	C
R	A

© Susan Marcuccio 2019

To *empower* means to shift the power back to the other person and allow them to come up with their own solutions. This helps to ensure that there are healthy boundaries in the relationship and each person takes responsibility for their own actions and response.

It's very easy to start to feel responsible for the other person and for them to become dependent on us. This is not helpful for either person.

Empowering someone (and avoiding trying to rescue them) builds their self-esteem so they feel good about themselves, rather than looking to us as the person 'saving' them.

We can feel compelled to want to rescue them and to try and fix the problem for them or give advice. If we can *empower* the person to come up with their own options and solutions while we simply journey alongside, it can help the person to not only take ownership but to feel good about themself.

Empowering the person to tap into their own coping mechanisms means that when we are not with them, they have these coping skills to draw on or other people in their world that can provide support.

In summary, practise using <u>all four parts</u> of the CARE Model within the boundaries of your role or anytime you want to walk alongside people and show you care. Remember: *connection, awareness, response* and *empower* all work together, not in isolation.

TWO MODELS USED TOGETHER

The CARE Model can also be used in conjunction with the Perspective Supervision Process Model, as shown in the overlay of the two models on the next page.

Perspective Supervision Process Model / CARE Model (Together)

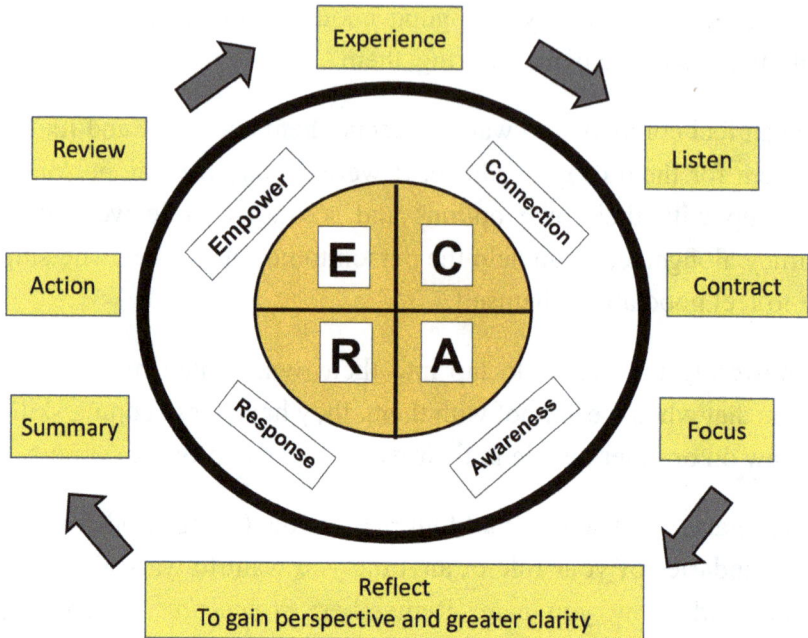

© Susan Marcuccio 2019

Using the two models together can assist with:

➡ making a connection (*during experience and listen*)

➡ having awareness (*as you contract, focus and reflect*)

➡ considering your response (*during summary and action*)

➡ remembering to empower (*through action and review*)

➡ keeping connection and awareness throughout the process (*in order to maintain the authentic, genuine relationship and not become too mechanical*)

Self-Care

Many people in the helping professions are great at caring for others but don't always care for themselves well. It's important to be aware of issues that can impact self-care and to also have some 'self-care strategies' to address these issues.

The SELF-CARE ISSUES AND STRATEGIES CHART can be used in supervision or mentoring or any other work situation where there is a focus on self-care. It's also suitable for anyone wanting to focus on their *own* self-care.

Caring for yourself is important! The chart below highlights some of the self-care issues that we can all face. Also listed are corresponding strategies which might be helpful to explore further:

◊ Self-Care Issues	◊ Self-Care Strategies
Poor time management	Improve time management
Boundary issues	Develop appropriate boundaries
Not being authentic	Take steps to live authentically
Trying to live up to others' expectations	Free yourself from others' expectations
Difficulties with transition from work to home / home to work	Smooth transitions from work to home / home to work

This chart is continued on next page…

SELF-CARE ISSUES AND STRATEGIES CHART continued…

◊ **Self-Care Issues**	◊ **Self-Care Strategies**
Emotional/physical/cognitive/spiritual tank/s drained	Refill emotional/physical/cognitive/ spiritual tank/s
Not dealing with emotional issues	Dealing with own emotional issues
Impacted by perfectionism	Tackle perfectionism
Unclear job roles	Gain clarity with job roles
Relationship tension	Resolve relationship tension
Unprocessed grief	Working through grief
Not recognising signs of stress and burnout	Improved awareness of signs of stress and burnout
Expectations are unrealistic / don't match reality	Working towards realistic expectations / matching reality
Relying wholly on ourselves / family	Spreading load / healthy support structures in place
No supervision or mentoring support (or inadequate support)	Good professional supervision and/or mentoring support in place

TRAFFIC LIGHTS TRIAGING TOOL

One way that I have found helpful in supervision to assist a person to gauge *how they are going* is using the 'Traffic Lights Triaging Tool'. This is a simple but yet profound way to invite a person to *really check* where they are in this moment but also in their life in general.

The Traffic Lights Triaging Tool is designed for use in supervision but can also be used for mentoring or chaplaincy or really for anyone to use to assist others. You can also use it for yourself to gain new perspectives on your *own* life and profession.

When someone is experiencing a difficult time, it can feel overwhelming. By stepping back and gaining a broader perspective, you can step out of your immediate situation for a moment and see the *bigger picture* more easily and with greater clarity.

⬦⬦⬦ Traffic Lights Triaging Tool

Red = Emergency

Yellow = Average

Green = Flourishing

© Susan Marcuccio 2019

To use the Traffic Light Triaging Tool, follow these steps:

Step one: Invite the person to look at the traffic light picture and choose one of the colours that represents where they feel they are right now, today, in this moment.

Are they:

> ➪ **green** – they are flourishing today
> ➪ **yellow** – they are feeling fairly average/normal
> ➪ **red** – it feels like they are in an emergency situation

The traffic light colours give the person something concrete to focus on rather than having abstract thoughts swirling through their head. Ask the person to write down the colour of the traffic light that they have chosen to represent how they feel right now.

Step two: Invite the person to now <u>lean back</u> in their seat, giving the feeling of 'stepping back' from their current situation. Then ask them the same question but this time, about their life *in general*.

Are they:

> ➪ **green** – they are flourishing in their life overall
> ➪ **yellow** – their life in general is fairly average/normal
> ➪ **red** – the big picture of their life is in an emergency state

Ask the person to write down the colour of the traffic light that they have chosen that best represents where they are in their *life overall*.

Whilst you are still in step two, consider whether it is helpful to give the person time to share some of what they are experiencing in their life (both right now and overall), particularly if they have indicated that they are in <u>red emergency</u>.

If you are using this tool in a supervision context, then honouring the story is important. However, make sure you leave enough time to follow all the steps so you both don't get stuck in the story. As shown earlier (in chapter four), it's important that you have the opportunity to enter the process of supervision.

Step three: Reflect together on the findings of steps one and two using the table on the opposite page. In other words, look at:

⇨ right now
⇨ life in general
⇨ the outcome of the <u>combination</u> of the two

Reflecting on these findings gives the person a simple *snapshot* of what's going on in their lives and how they are *really* doing.

I have found that sometimes, a person comes in, and they are in an emergency situation right now but once they realise that their life in general is flourishing, it helps them to see a broader perspective of their life.

If the person is flourishing now <u>and</u> in general, then that is cause for celebration!

However, if they are in an emergency state right now <u>and</u> in a general emergency state, then there may be a need for immediate action as well as a longer-term plan.

If they are in average now and overall, then it is a good opportunity for reflection with the aim to look for ways to flourish.

Here are some possible combinations of right now and life in general:

Right Now	Life in General	Outcome	Possible Action
Red	Red	Emergency both now and in general	Immediate action may be required - may need to refer
Red	Yellow	Emergency now but average in general	Deal with immediate emergency and plan to work on moving life in general to flourishing
Red	Green	Emergency now but flourishing in general	Deal with immediate emergency but remind them that in general they are flourishing
Yellow	Red	Average now but emergency in general	Reflect on what is happening right now but see if action is needed in general
Yellow	Yellow	Average now and average in general	Look at ways to move from average to flourishing both now and in general
Yellow	Green	Average now but flourishing in general	Celebrate person flourishing in general but reflect on what is happening now
Green	Red	Flourishing now but emergency in general	Reflect on what is going so well right now but see if action is needed in general
Green	Yellow	Flourishing now but average in general	Reflect on what is going so well now and how to move to flourishing in whole life
Green	Green	Flourishing now and in general	Celebrate together and work on how to keep it like this

Step Four: Look at the possible action column and see what is required based on the outcome of the activity. There may be action items that are required *right now*, or it could be that something can be worked on *over time*.

Remember to stay in your role and refer if required. It may be that just assisting the person to have this broader perspective will give them clarity on their situation and empower them to take the necessary action required.

Additional Steps: You can also use the Traffic Light Triaging Tool in conjunction with the Three Ringed Model (from Chapter Three) by looking at each area of a person's life individually.

You can ask the person to use the Traffic Light Triaging Tool for their personal life, work life and spiritual life. This allows the person to look at where they are at specifically, right now and in general, for each area (personal, work, spiritual). For the supervisor or person in the support role, using the two approaches together helps to see when referral might be needed (including appropriate referral pathways).

THREE RINGED MODEL: Personal Life / Work Life / Spiritual Life

Your Personal Life

Your Work Life

Your Spiritual Life

© Susan Marcuccio 2013

Sit back and think of your life <u>right now</u> - is it red, yellow or green?

➡ Consider your *Personal Life* right now - is it red/yellow/green?

➡ What about your *Work Life* right now - is it red/yellow/green?

➡ How is your *Spiritual Life* right now - is it red/yellow/green?

Now, sit back and think of your life <u>in general</u> - is it red/yellow/green?

➡ Consider your *Personal Life* in general - is it red/yellow/green?

➡ What about your *Work Life* in general - is it red/yellow/green?

➡ How is your *Spiritual Life* in general - is it red/yellow/ green?

As you can see there are many different ways to use the Traffic Light Triaging Tool - just choose what is right for the person and the situation.

THE ENHANCE MODEL

The ENHANCE Model outlines elements (such as being 'attuned', 'nourished' or 'energised') that I have found in my experience to be helpful for holistic health and wellness. That is, having these elements present in your life can result in the enhancement of certain aspects of personal and professional life.

The ENHANCE Model

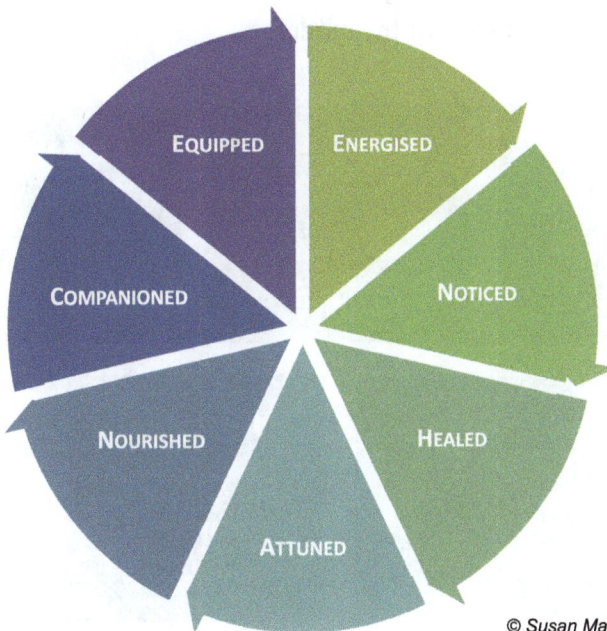

© Susan Marcuccio 2022

For example, if we take the element 'attuned' I am referring to the benefits that come if you personally and professionally:

➪ *live in harmony with*
➪ *be aware of*
➪ *live consistently* with

your values, principles, beliefs and calling.

The model can be used by anyone in any context to identify the elements that are already present in a person's life as well as identifying elements that would benefit from further development or 'enhancement'.

The ENHANCE Model recognises that in order for you to flourish in your profession and your personal life, you may need to put some time into working on certain elements. You *can* do this work on your own, however I have found that supervision provides a supportive environment and structured process to address each of the areas covered in the 7 elements of the model.

Energized
To gain energy, capacity, abundance, vitality, drive, zeal, endurance, strength, stamina and toughness.

Noticed
To be seen and heard, to have someone notice any red flags and assist with processing the experiences.

Healed
To be whole, integrated, restored, settled and well - body, soul, spirit - physically, spiritually, emotionally, cognitively.

Attuned
In harmony with, to be aware of and living consistently with values, principles, beliefs and calling.

Nourished
To gain life, health and growth, be encouraged, championed, built up strengthened, comforted and supported.

Companioned
Accompanied, a confidential space to be heard, not alone, to have a place to connect.

Equipped
To have what is needed for the role, to learn, to be aware, to gain skills, to be ready.

© Susan Marcuccio 2022

These boxes can be used along with the pie chart (on the previous page) when working to ENHANCE your own or another person's personal and professional life.

If we now look at each element more closely, you will see questions posed to assist you or the person you are working with to reflect and take any action required.

Energised

In order to thrive in your life and profession you need to make sure that what you are doing energises you! Life is too short to settle for a life that is just going through the motions or to pay the bills.

Of course, you need to make good choices for the season that you are in but connecting in with your passion, your calling, and doing something meaningful gives you that energy to bounce out of bed in the morning.

Being energised gives you stamina, greater capacity, you have that zeal, and drive to keep going despite any obstacles. It helps you to have endurance, to go the distance and have mental toughness.

Are you living a life that energises you?

Noticed

I wonder who is looking out for you? Who are you letting into your life and giving the right to speak into it? Is there someone in your life that will notice any red flags, that you may have gone off course, or heading in a direction that may be detrimental for you?

We all need to have at least one person that is noticing us, speaking the truth to us and helping us process the experiences that we are having, in order to be healthy and thriving.

Healed

Are you taking stock of your life, body, soul and spirit? Are you working to ensure that you have good health in all these areas and are working though any issues that arise and working towards healing in every area of your life?

Are you monitoring yourself physically, spiritually, emotionally and cognitively to ensure that each area has plenty of reserves, so you are giving out from your overflow not from a place of deficit?

Are you living an integrated and authentic life where you are able to be yourself in all environments with just the appropriate amount of persona? Are you working on the areas that need restoration?

Attuned

Have you spent time really getting to know what your values are? Do you know what principles you live your life by? Are you in harmony with, and living consistently with your values, principles, beliefs and calling?

As you become more aware of, attentive and responsive to these areas in your life, you become more attuned to things being out of order and this prompts you to make changes.

When we try and live our lives and we are not attuned to what is going on, we can miss important signs and promptings that can eventually lead us away from a flourishing life.

Nourished

We all need people in our life that are championing us on, those who will encourage us, build us up, comfort us when we are down and support us when we need it. I wonder who you have in your life that is doing this? It helps us to keep going, to push forward to grow and take risks, someone who believes in us when we stop believing in ourselves.

A firm safe foundation, that nourishes us and give us life and vitality. We all need this in our lives. Who do you have that is doing that for you?

Companioned

As we all walk through this journey of life, we need to have people to walk alongside us, to accompany us as we navigate the many twists and turns that our life can take.

There is benefit in having someone who is separate from our world that can be impartial and has no agenda. This can allow us to open up about how we are really feeling and to discuss those things that we are grappling with without feeling judged.

It's so important to have a place to go where we can connect with someone with healthy boundaries and to know we are not alone. Do you have that person in your life?

Equipped

We all need to be equipped for the roles that we have or want to have, to be continually learning and growing. To have what is needed for your role, to learn to be aware, gain skills, be transformed, to be ready to step into your unique calling and purpose.

What steps are you taking to gain the skills you need. What steps are you taking to be the person you need to be? Be strategic, plan out the training and upskilling you need.

Think ahead and start to engage in transformational learning. Be equipped for all you need now and plan ahead for what you will need in the future. Who is helping you map this out? Get equipped and get going!

Spend time working on the elements that will ENHANCE your personal and professional life.

If you have read through this activity and you don't have someone to assist you in these areas, then consider contacting a supervisor or mentor and meeting with them, ideally on a monthly basis. You are your best asset:

You are worth investing in!

⟡ ⟡ ⟡

CHAPTER SEVEN

WORLDVIEW, VISION AND VALUES

This is what I believe
It keeps me safe in the world
I can explain the way things are
Let me be
Don't try and change me
Don't challenge my assumptions

What I need is a place to explore
Where you don't judge me
A place to take a risk
To look again
To see it differently
To gain new perspectives

Then I might ask you
What you believe
I can trust you
You have no agenda
Except to be with me
And show me respect

Above the Line, Below the Line

One day, I had a huge revelation:

Other people don't see the world the same as I do.

Now I am sure you are probably thinking:

"That's really obvious. Of course *I know* that other people don't see the world the same as I do."

However, on this particular day, it went beyond 'the obvious'. It was like my eyes were opened and I had a *much deeper understanding* that people experience life differently to me.

It suddenly all made so much sense!

Do you ever watch the way someone reacts or responds in a situation and ask yourself:

"Why did they do that?"

or

"I cannot fathom why they think that would be an appropriate way to behave in that situation."

It hit me: I was experiencing *their* situations through *my* filter.

My filter is the lens that I see the world through: *my worldview*. All the experiences that I have had over my life, good and bad, life-giving and challenging, have all come together to influence my *worldview*.

Even if someone has had a similar experience to me, they still have multiple factors that mean they experience it differently. We each can only see situations from our *own perspective*, through our own lens, our own filter. We can *attempt* to see and understand what it's like for someone else through empathy or we can ask the person to tell us what it's like for them but still, we don't really know how they are experiencing the situation.

Having this revelation was life changing for me. From that point forward, I began to view other people's actions very differently and tried my best to imagine what it might be like to see things from *someone else's perspective*.

When I hear of people doing terrible things to another person, I think to myself:

"I wonder what has happened to that person in their life such that, when they found themselves in this situation, they made *that choice?*"

or

"What immobilised them to <u>not</u> act in a *different way?*"

When you start to view other people in the world this way, it helps you to not be so judgemental. It doesn't mean that what the person has done is okay, but what it does mean is that you withhold your judgement and take the time to wonder about:

⇨ what experiences they have had in their life
⇨ how they see the world
⇨ what it is like for them

A common situation that I see quite a lot was brought to me by a particular supervisee. She explained that she was really struggling with someone on her team at work. She just couldn't understand why the other person was not behaving in what she felt was an appropriate way to act in a work setting.

The supervisee felt the person had been given plenty of opportunities, perhaps even more than others. The supervisee was this person's leader and she expressed that she had given the person lots of mentoring and had offered praise around the work they had done. Even so, her team member was just not stepping up to the mark the way she expected that they should.

My supervisee said she was feeling really angry with her team member and just didn't know what to do...

I have found that when someone is feeling angry, there is usually something that is under the anger, such as frustration, hurt or fear. It can be helpful to identify which of these it is. Sometimes it becomes evident that the person is actually experiencing two or three of these emotions.

I shared about the feelings that can be *under* anger with my supervisee and asked her if she was feeling frustration, hurt or fear in regards to this situation. She gave it some thought and said:

"I feel really frustrated. They are not making the most of the opportunities I am giving them."

The supervisee then went on to say:

"It's so annoying. Don't they know how good they have it?"

I continued to listen to the supervisee as she expressed herself about the situation:

"I could easily have chosen someone else, but I really felt so sure that they had the potential to really rise in their leadership. I thought they could take more responsibility but no... They are just throwing it all away!"

I could really feel the anger as she spoke. Then she went on to say:

"I am feeling really hurt that I have put myself out there for this person and now they are not showing any loyalty. All the time that I have put in now seems wasted."

I took a moment to validate the emotions that my supervisee was expressing. At this point in the interaction:

➡ I could have given my opinion
➡ I could have said what I thought
➡ I could have given advice
➡ I could have told her what a good way forward could be

I could have BUT - I didn't.

I have learnt that, while it can be tempting to do so, simply giving my opinion is not helping the person to see the situation with fresh eyes for themselves. Also, my opinion is just that – an opinion, which may not even be correct.

It is much more effective to simply provide a place for the supervisee to explore the situation and reflect in a way that they may see it more clearly for themselves and from a different perspective.

If a supervisee has their own revelation or 'aha' moment then transformational learning is taking place: it changes *who they are* and the way that they *see the world*, and their own *worldview* is expanded. This is much more helpful and powerful and empowering than simply being given advice.

The next step I took with my supervisee was to suggest that we look at an activity…

Together, we decided to reflect on the situation about the team member using the 'Above the Line, Below the Line' activity. We started by just using the left-hand column (**what they say and do / who they are**).

Above the Line, Below the Line

Understanding who the person is, what you are not seeing, and what may be going on for them..

Above the line - what they say and do	Above the line - what you say and do
Reactions, responses, comments	Reactions, responses, comments
What you see, hear and observe	*What they see, hear and observe*

Below the line - who they are	Below the line - who you are
Their worldview, values, beliefs	Your worldview, values, beliefs
What gives their life meaning	What gives your life meaning
What is important to them	What is importance to you
Their experiences	Your experiences
What you don't see or hear	*What they don't see or hear*

© Susan Marcuccio 2018

First of all, I asked my supervisee to draw a horizontal line on the page. On top of the line, I asked her to write the words: **Above the Line** and then, in that position, to write all the things that she had seen the person do or had heard them say that were relevant to this situation. Basically, I asked her what she had observed about the person.

Our <u>observations</u> are all we really have to go by when we are interacting with people. People share with us as much as they feel comfortable to. So, we have the information they share and the behaviours we observe. From a combination of the two, we then tend to make judgements about the person.

I then asked my supervisee to write the words **Below the Line** underneath the line. However, before I asked her to write anything in that lower position, we went on to discuss what *below the line* really means.

Below the line is all the things about the person that we don't see or hear <u>overtly</u>. It's what is going on <u>covertly</u> for a person. It's what informs the lens that they look through when they see the world. It is made up of their beliefs, their assumptions about the world and life in general.

Below the line is:

⇨ a mixture of all the experiences that a person has had

⇨ the things that they have been told

⇨ the things they have learnt about life

⇨ what gives their life meaning

⇨ what they value

⇨ what is important to them

All the things *below the line* make up the person's worldview. Their worldview, that is, the way they see the world, is also influenced by culture and family and other influential people in their life.

So, when we are observing a person and hearing them talk, all of what is happening *above the line*, comes from *below the line*.

Once we had spent time discussing what *below the line* really means, I asked my supervisee to write down all the relevant things that she knew about the person that she could now see were from *below the line*.

My supervisee then looked at me and said:

"I have no idea about these things. I don't know."

We sat in silence for a few moments until she said:

"Wow, I didn't even think about any of this."

We then spent the next part of the supervision session with my supervisee considering the aspects that were from *below the line* regarding their team member.

After a while, we stopped and reflected on what we had done so far in the session. I checked in and asked her where she was at. Her countenance seemed to have changed and I asked her how she was now feeling. She said that she was no longer feeling angry with her team member. She realised that there was a whole lot more going on for her that she hadn't been aware of or hadn't even really considered.

I asked her if she was now feeling empathy for her team member, and she answered with:

"Yes!"

We then spoke about how empathy is a great way to gauge how we are feeling about a situation.

If we <u>don't have</u> empathy for a person, then it's a good indication that something has triggered us, and we are dealing with what's going on <u>for us</u> rather than considering what's going on for the other person.

It was as we slowed it down and my supervisee felt safe enough to explore the situation, that she saw it more clearly. She was then able to get a real sense of what was happening in the situation and what she needed to do next.

This all happened without me giving advice or giving my opinion. In fact, all I did was assist the supervisee to enter into the process of supervision. To recap the process (from Chapter Four), the steps we took were:

➡ I listened to the story (*experience*)

➡ We *contracted* what we would work with <u>on this day</u>

➡ We got a clear *focus* (feelings of anger and frustration)

➡ We used an activity to enter the *reflective space* (in order to see the situation from a new perspective)

➡ We *summarised* where she was at (shifted to empathy)

➡ She got a sense of what she needed to do next (*action*)

➡ We *reviewed* what the process had been like

As the supervisor, a key part of my role was being able to think about what my supervisee had brought to supervision on that day and to then offer an appropriate exercise (in this case 'Above the Line, Below the Line').

I chose this particular resource on this day because I thought it may assist my supervisee to see with more clarity, from a new perspective - *which it did!!*

I use the Above the Line, Below the Line activity in many different situations as I find it to be so helpful and also enlightening. So far, in the example above, we have only used the left-hand side where the wording is about the *other person*. If we look at the activity again, we can see that the right-hand side assists us to go through the same steps but this time, *thinking about ourselves.*

⬦ Above the Line, Below the Line

Understanding who the person is, what you are not seeing, and what may be going on for them..

Above the line - what they say and do
Reactions, responses, comments
What you see, hear and observe

Below the line - who they are
Their worldview, values, beliefs
What gives their life meaning
What is important to them
Their experiences
What you don't see or hear

Above the line - what you say and do
Reactions, responses, comments
What they see, hear and observe

Below the line - who you are
Your worldview, values, beliefs
What gives your life meaning
What is importance to you
Your experiences
What they don't see or hear

© Susan Marcuccio 2018

In the session with my supervisee, we looked at the activity again, this time by going through the steps using the right-hand column. This gave her the opportunity to also look at her own **Above the Line, Below the Line**.

When we use the activity this way (using left <u>and</u> right columns) we have the opportunity to experience self-reflection. Also, to realise:

The other person also only knows what they see, hear and observe <u>overtly</u> for you (your above the line)! They don't see or hear or know about what's going on <u>covertly</u> for you (your below the line).

From the process of supervision, my supervisee gained new perspectives on what might be happening *below the line* for the person in her team. She also experienced changes and gained a deeper understanding of what was going on for herself *below the line*.

*Changes that occur **below the line** influence how we live our lives **above the line**. That is, when our worldview changes, we alter what we say and do (our reactions, comments and responses).*

Let's take a moment to consider what might have happened if my supervisee hadn't brought this situation to supervision and hadn't had the opportunity to process the situation and to feel heard and validated?

What would have happened with the anger that she felt?

Also, I wonder what it would have been like for the team member to have felt the anger from her leader and the pressure that she may have felt from the expectations that her leader had of her?

Now let's think about the impact that the process of supervision session may have had: *I wonder how the relationship might be going now that the supervisee is considering the situation from the team member's perspective?*

Imagine if we all had the opportunity to slow down, to be shown that sometimes, we jump to quick conclusions. How would life change, for ourselves and those we interact with, if we all had the insight needed to consider how other people see and experience the world?

I have a further example to share of someone feeling frustrated about another person's behaviour. They came to see me for a supervision session and told me that they were a chaplain. As I listened to their story, I became aware that he was frustrated as he couldn't seem to get a person he was visiting to open up and share more deeply about the situation he was facing. I listened to him talk about how frustrating that was for my supervisee and the sense he had that he was not really able to *do his job*.

I asked the supervisee to tell me what they were doing when they were with the person. He shared that they seemed to have good visits and that the gentleman asked for him to go and see him regularly. His frustration was that they rarely got past surface things like the weather, what was happening in the world and other seemingly unimportant topics.

As a chaplain, he really felt that they should be talking about spiritual things and about what the person believed as the person was very sick and could possibly die soon. However, the person just *shut down* every time they went near the subject of faith.

On this day, we reflected on the question of how he could tell that he was doing his job well. In other words, what were his expectations for providing 'successful' chaplaincy visits.

He thought about what his perception was of the encounters he was having with this gentleman. I then asked the question:

"What do you think he wants from you?"

The chaplain said:

"I think he feels some comfort when I am there with him in the room. I get a sense that he feels very alone and although he has a faith, he doesn't want to talk about it."

I responded:

"Do you think he is settled in his beliefs?"

"Well, I don't really know," he answered, "as he doesn't talk about his beliefs. But he seems to light up when I visit, and it feels like the room becomes peaceful and calm."

"So," I followed up with, "having you there as the 'God' person seems to bring him peace and calm?"

"Yes!" he answered.

The chaplain then had an 'aha moment' and a realisation that he <u>was</u> actually doing the role of a chaplain and <u>was</u> doing what most people can't do. He was staying in the moment with this gentleman and not pushing his own agenda. He was doing what was really needed – allowing the gentleman to 'have the God person there'.

We all have a set of beliefs that helps us to be okay in the world, and a set of assumptions that mean we can explain the world around us. When we are feeling fragile, we often can't risk discussing our beliefs, as it threatens to *unravel us*.

People can be in a situation where they are using all their energy to just be 'okay in the world'. They can't challenge their beliefs and assumptions as they are relying on what they currently think to keep them safe.

As chaplains, our role is to be with someone and not push them to talk about what we think they need to or should talk about. Our role as a chaplain is to create a safe non-judgmental space for people to share, if they want to, but not to push them.

What a gift we give someone to just *be there with them*, with no agenda but to *be with them* and to be available to talk about the hard subjects - if <u>they</u> want to.

Ironically, it may seem as though this is a very passive approach, but it is mostly the <u>only way</u> a person will actually consider changing their beliefs.

Changing Beliefs

In the context of supervision and mentoring, we need to be very mindful of where someone is at regarding *their beliefs*.

Learning is an important part of supervision and mentoring, so we may have contracted together to discuss beliefs and challenge assumptions and to engage in transformational learning around this area. However, we need to go *gently*, providing a safe place for people, to support them if and when they feel *brave enough* to really look at what they believe. Only then will they be in a position to tackle any cognitive dissonance that they may be facing.

Cognitive dissonance is when we are presented with information that challenges the current belief we have. We cannot stay too long in a state of dissonance, so we try and resolve it. We do this in one of the following ways:

➪ Completely dismissing the new information, even if there is compelling evidence to back it up

or

➪ Examining the new information and integrating it into our current belief system

or

➪ Examining the new information and changing our existing beliefs

You have probably met people who hang on to a belief or assumption regardless of how absurd it may seem to others but it's what they have decided to believe in order for them to be okay in the world. If we simply challenge them, they will usually just dig in deeper.

Often the only way for a person to have the courage to really look at a currently held belief in order to consider other options is when they feel like they are safe.

What do I mean by safe in this context?

➡ When they are with someone who <u>respects them</u> and <u>their right</u> to have whatever beliefs they have

➡ When someone gives them space to explore and doesn't jump in while they are in a vulnerable state

➡ When someone doesn't try and push their own beliefs onto the person

In my experience, only when a person is feeling safe will they open up enough to really examine their beliefs.

It is such a privilege to be with someone when they are considering changing their beliefs.

Sometimes, a 'challenge' to currently held beliefs is thrust upon someone. This might happen when something occurs that *shatters their worldview*, causing them to enter this state unwillingly.

For example, a person who has received a terminal cancer diagnosis is suddenly confronted by the realisation that their life expectancy is limited. As this person faces the reality of their own death, they may have to unwillingly let go of some of their long-held beliefs about their life.

Having someone with you as you 'let go' of your existing beliefs or 'acknowledge' that the beliefs that have kept you safe are now shattered and therefore no longer available, can make all the difference. This is a compelling argument for the need for supervisors, mentors and chaplains who are trained to be able to 'hold the space' for people who are experiencing this.

Vision and values are another important aspect of how we see and experience the world and are therefore the next topic I will delve into.

How Values and Vision Influence Your Life

I am a visionary. The moment I wake up in the morning until the minute I fall asleep, I am dreaming, planning, visioning, and having multiple ideas.

Being a visionary gives me energy, excitement, and a feeling like I used to get when I was a child, and I was going to a birthday party after school. All day I would be so excited I could scream. I just couldn't wait to get there.

I still get that feeling now when I have an idea and start to put it into practice: I can't wait to get there! I usually have at least a 10-year plan and have devised a strategy of how I will get to where I'm hoping to go.

I used to think that everyone needed to be like me and have a plan and a strategy. If I came across someone without a plan, I would start to work with them to get a vision for their life.

One day I had a revelation - there is another way to live... Rather than being *vision driven*, some people are more *values driven*.

One of the down sides to being *vision driven* is that it is hard to live in the moment. You get so fixated on the vision ahead that you are not present in the moment.

Those who are *values driven* live each day according to their values. They live in each moment and as the day unfolds, they do what is in front of them and consistent with their values. For instance, someone may have 'compassion' as a high value.

A person that is *values driven* will make choices based on that value. If they were to reflect on their day and they had shown compassion, then the day was a success.

To someone who is more *vision driven,* if they haven't done something that day that was working towards the vision then the day would not be considered a success.

Now of course, you can be vision driven <u>and</u> values driven however, in my experience, people tend to lean more towards one or the other.

If we are more *vision* focused or driven, then even if we are not aware of it, our *vision* usually comes <u>out of our values</u>.

For someone who is both vision <u>and</u> values driven but leans more towards vision, they may hold 'compassion' as a high value but not stop what they are doing to show compassion to someone.

When we look at the reason for them not stopping, we find that they *chose* to not stop and help.

Why didn't they stop and show compassion when compassion is of high value to them?

Stopping would have <u>prevented</u> them from doing *in that moment* what was needed to work towards their vision.

What is their vision?

Their vision is of a future time when many would be helped and shown compassion. Their focus is on the *vision of helping many* rather than on the *value of helping one person* on that particular day.

⬌⬍ Values & Vision Tool

1. Are you VALUES driven?

2. Are you VISION driven?

3. Are you both VALUES & VISION driven?

4. Where are you on both these scales?

HIGH	VALUES	LOW

HIGH	VISION	LOW

© Susan Marcuccio 2021

Values and vision can impact you personally, but also influence you professionally.

What do we do if the profession we have chosen is not consistent with our values or does not take us towards our vision?

➡ We may leave and pursue something that is more in line with our vision and values

or

➡ We might slowly lose our passion and settle for much less that we were made for

One of the reasons I love supervision is that it helps people to stop and consider what they are doing with their life, both personally and professionally. I believe that *all people* have a calling - the very thing that they were created to do. Being connected to our calling means we have at least some vision for our life even if we don't have a long-term vision like those who are vision focused or vision driven.

How sad that some people never find their calling and live a life with no real purpose or meaning. If you are looking for way to find your calling (or assist someone else), you might like to revisit the 'Connecting to your Calling' activity in Chapter One. This activity can be used to assist you to identify your calling as well as more clearly identify your values.

Values and Vision in Supervision

As a supervisor, your vision will influence:

➡ how you plan for your sessions

➡ your overall plan for your supervision role/business

➡ where you are heading in the future

I had a vision for supervision which included establishing a supervision and mentoring program as well as running my own supervision business. I have been very strategic and intentional, training to be a supervisor, aligning myself with those leading the way in supervision, networking, studying and continually learning all I can on the subject.

What I have discovered is that you can try and be good at *lots of things* or you can find that *one thing* that you are called to do and just focus on becoming an expert in that *one area*.

I started with just one supervisee and then progressed to seeing three to four people on a Saturday morning while still working fulltime in another job. I then cut down to working three days per week in my other job and giving two full days to my private supervision business.

Eventually I was able to just focus on supervision. That is, being a supervisor in my own private practice, running a supervision and mentoring program, teaching supervision and running supervision workshops.

I'm always looking for ways to upskill myself, get more experience and be on the cutting edge of what's happening in the supervision world.

I'm living the dream - but as I am a visionary, I'm not stopping there...

Vision Focused

Being a visionary does influence how I run a supervision session. If you are vision focused, you might identity with the same sorts of issues and experiences that I continue to be mindful of.

For example, I love working in models to ensure that the process of supervision happens. I naturally approach a supervision session with the <u>end in mind</u>:

"What does that person want to walk away with from this session?" is the question that is at the forefront for me.

While that is a good question to have as a supervisor, I need to be careful that I am also mindful of the role of values in a session.

For example, I need to hold to the value of being *truly present in the moment* with my supervisee.

Also, to remember the values I have, such as:

➡ respect
➡ being non-judgmental
➡ having compassion
➡ really caring (within the boundaries of my role)

I have learnt that the relationship is so important and can be lost if I just focus on what we want to <u>achieve</u> in a session. I'm thankful that when I trained to be a chaplain and then entered chaplaincy ministry, I learnt the importance of being *fully present in the moment.*

I had some amazing teachers. When I say 'teachers', I'm actually referring to the people that I had the privilege of *walking alongside* or *sitting with in their pain.*

Being in the moment was the very thing that I struggled with in those early days. I became aware of its importance through engaging in my own supervision and reflecting on my encounters with the people I sat with. I'm pleased to say that *being in the moment* eventually became a strength and I can now sit with someone and be truly with them, fully present whenever *the moment* needs this of me. It is however, something that I find beneficial to continue working on, to avoid any complacency setting in and to ensure I work through any trigger points that might arise.

Values Focused

Being values focused can mean that in a supervision session, you might have a tendency to 'lose you way' as you are not as mindful of seeing the session as a whole. You will likely be more focused on the supervisory relationship and wanting to make sure that the way you are approaching the session is congruent with what's important to you.

Once you have thought about whether you are vision focused or values focused (or both), you may want to ask yourself these questions:

➡ How do VALUES influence my provision of supervision in relation to...

- Planning for the whole year?
- Running each individual supervision session?

➡ How does VISION influence my provision of supervision in relation to...

- Planning for the whole year?
- Running each individual supervision session?

If you are not a supervisor however you run mentoring sessions or other types of interactions in your professional role, you could also ask yourself these questions. For example:

➡ How do VALUES influence my provision of mentoring* in relation to...

- Planning for the whole year?
- Running each individual mentoring session?

➡ How does VISION influence my provision of mentoring* in relation to...

- Planning for the whole year?
- Running each individual mentoring session?

Feel free to insert 'other professional role' in place of mentoring to make this relevant to you.

I have developed an activity using this concept of vision and values which can assist people to see how they can use both vision and values to get a bigger picture of their life and gain a broader perspective. To complete this activity, you will need to be holding a book (*it can be any book as the book is just there to represent the overall concept of the activity*).

This activity can be completed by yourself (on your own) or can be used in a supervision session or other context where you are assisting someone else to look at their vision and values.

VISION AND VALUES ACTIVITY:

Step One: Hold up a book in your hand. As you are holding the book, imagine that it represents your life. In this book, there are chapters. Think about your life right now. You are currently in one of the chapters.

Step Two: At the top of a piece of A4 landscape paper, write the present year (for example, 2022). The piece of paper represents the chapter of the book that you are currently in.

Step Three: Along the bottom of the page, draw four lines that you can write words on. Spread the lines evenly across the bottom of the whole page. These lines represent YOUR VALUES.

To get ready to write your values on the lines, think about the four top values that you would like to have run through *your whole book.*

If you are unsure of what your top four values are, you may like to refer to the tool we explored in Chapter One (Connecting to Your Calling).

Write your top four values on the lines – <u>one value per line</u>.

Step Four: On the rest of the page, there is room to draw some pictures. Think about what pictures you would like to include. Don't worry if you don't consider yourself to be good at drawing – even line drawings, symbols or rough sketches are fine.

The drawings represent each of the items that you are currently doing or want to include in this current chapter (the year you are in). The drawings are your vision for this time in your life.

For example, you might draw:

- ➡ a holiday destination
- ➡ spending time with family
- ➡ a sport you play (or want to play)
- ➡ a new purchase you're hoping to make
- ➡ a course you are undertaking (or hoping to enrol in)
- ➡ financial plans such as a savings goal
- ➡ your current work role/s and/or work aspirations
- ➡ anything else that you want to add…

Remember this is *your* page so add the things which *you* have a vision about for this year. The list is YOUR LIST so add the things that are part of YOUR VISION.

When someone is writing a novel, they introduce characters early on in a book in readiness for future events that might happen. So, think about what else you might need to include now in order to set things up for future chapters.

For example, you may need to start studying in 'this chapter' in order to graduate in a 'future chapter'.

Step Five: At this step, look at the pictures you have drawn and decide which things you have influence over and which things are outside your control.

There may be some drawings that are actually a combination of the two (you have influence over some aspects but some aspects are outside your control).

Circle the pictures that you have some control over – these are your INFLUENCE GOALS - the things that you have influence over.

Put a square around the pictures that you have no control over - FAITH GOALS - these are things that you are hoping for but are outside your control.

If possible, it's good to have a balance of the two. Otherwise, you could find yourself with either:

➪ all goals that you have influence over, meaning that you are not being stretched

or

➪ all goals that are outside of your control, meaning that you may be setting yourself up for disappointment

Step Six: Now that you have filled out the A4 piece of paper, take a moment to reflect on what you have discovered about your vision and values.

This is a good opportunity to see if your vision (the pictures) and your values (the four words along the bottom) are aligned.

Are they closely aligned or would you like to make any adjustments?

Step Seven: Now you are ready to form an action plan. Your action plan is based on:

⮕ your VISION (pictures)

⮕ your VALUES (written along the bottom)

⮕ your INFLUENCE and FAITH goals (circles and squares)

What steps do you need to take now to ensure that the vision in this chapter will be realised?

For example, it might be to book the holiday that you have drawn or find out more about how to enrol in the training course.

You might feel confident to write your own action plan or if you are looking for ideas or structure, you could take something like this to a supervisor or mentor to discuss further.

If you are helping someone else to complete this activity, you could assist them to access information about different ways to write an action plan.

As we finish up with the book analogy, it's good to remember that we all have different chapters in our lives. Some chapters might be filled with activity, other chapters may be more for resting and recovery.

Whilst we don't have to have <u>everything</u> that we want to do in life (our vision) in <u>every</u> chapter, it's important to ensure that our values are a constant throughout the whole book.

Completing this vision and values activity may have helped you to gain new perspectives on the way that your values and visions align.

You may also now have greater clarity on the following:

➡ The current chapter you have just worked on is only one part of the whole book…

➡ Any other chapter (past or future) can be viewed as being just one part of the whole book…

➡ What you do in the current chapter in relation to your vision sets up opportunities to realise your vision in future chapters…

When you get to the end of the book (your life), will you have lived a life consistent with your values <u>and</u> having achieved your vision?

I find it to be helpful to go through this vision and values activity on a regular basis. It could even form part of a yearly review on your vision and values and how they are aligned.

Another important consideration as we plan for the future is the continued need for personal and professional growth and development which is a fundamental part of supervision.

Personal and Professional Growth and Development

Some of the saddest situations I hear about are when people are given leadership or management positions and responsibility even though they are not personally or professionally equipped to handle the role.

People may be keen or available for a leadership/management role or others may see potential in them, but often they find themselves thrown into a position that they are not ready for, with no clear plan in place for them to grow and develop as required.

The chart below shows two lines. A rise in leadership and/or responsibility line (orange) and a personal/professional growth and development line (purple).

As a person rises in leadership/responsibility (orange line), they need to track as close as they can with their growth and development (purple line). That is, they need just the right amount of challenge but not so much that they are 'out of their depth'.

Ideally, the two lines should be close together and on a similar trajectory. That is, growth and development follow closely just under the requirements of the role. When this occurs, the person in the role rises up to meet what's expected from them, thereby growing and developing personally and professionally at the right rate to not be overwhelmed but equally, not be underchallenged.

Personal & Professional Development

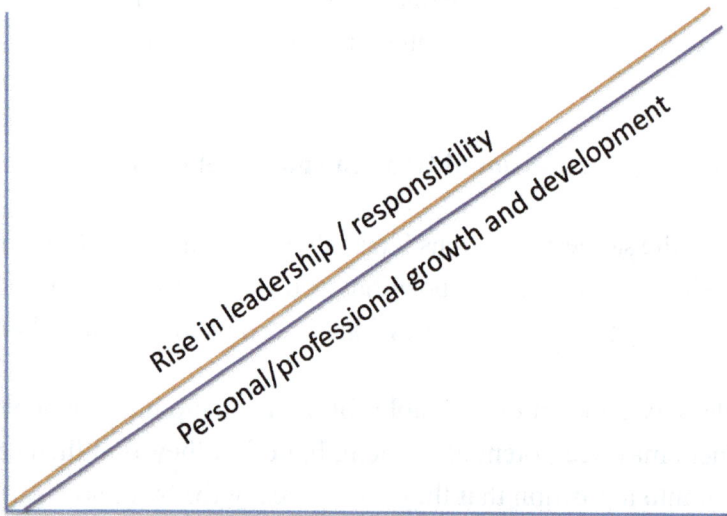

Rise in leadership / responsibility

Personal/professional growth and development

© Susan Marcuccio 2015

Now let's look at the second chart where there is a growing gap between the two lines.

⬧ Personal & Professional Development

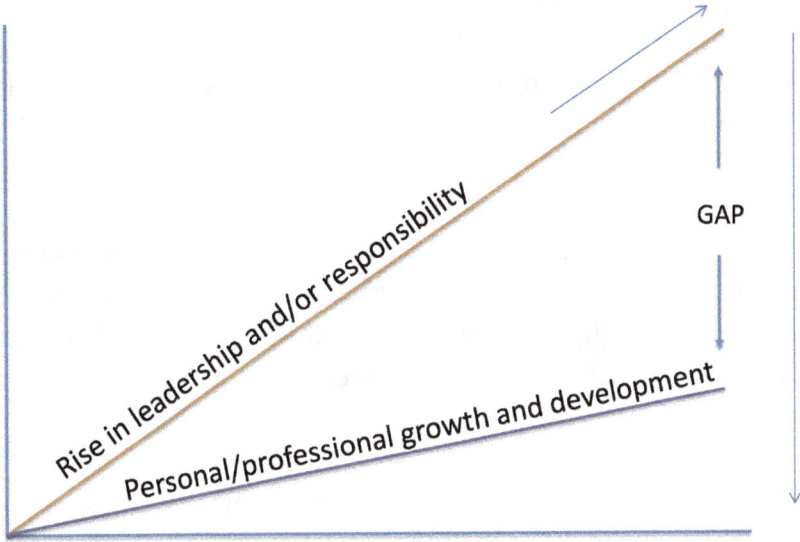

Rise in leadership and/or responsibility

Personal/professional growth and development

GAP

If the person is not growing and developing personally and professionally at the level required for the role and responsibility, then there is a widening gap.

If this gap is not addressed, the person can end up having a spectacular fall (represented by the downward pointing arrow on the right-hand side).

What tends to happen is the person tries to lead at the level required and tries to become the person they need to be, which can be exhausting and emotionally depleting. In order to do this, they have to put on a *huge persona*, so they are not able to live authentically or just be themselves.

I'm all for being stretched outside your comfort zone and working to reach your potential. In fact, you need a level of challenge to become all you were designed to be.

What I'm talking about in the second chart, however, is when it is just *too much of a rise*, <u>too quickly,</u> and the person just does not have the maturity to function at this higher level for any length of time.

This can have devastating results. The person can try and live up to the expectations and may even be able to bluff their way for a while. Over time though, the result can be that they 'burn out' or end up living in a state of constant stress which might cause damage to their health.

Sometimes the person uses whatever means they can to try and stay afloat. This can include overuse of alcohol, or inappropriate use of drugs or extra marital affairs or really anything to help them cover up that they are not coping. In some cases, it can also lead to self-destructive behaviours.

People who find themselves out of their depth in their role at work often feel that they can't say anything to their manager as it could put their job in jeopardy, or they can feel they would be letting down the person who believed in them.

This is one of the reason's it's so important that people have someone external to be able to talk to about the situation they find themselves in.

*If you find <u>yourself</u> in this position, **please speak up** – find someone you trust that you can talk to openly.*

A supervisor or mentor can provide a safe confidential space for the person to share how they are feeling and to be honest if they are not coping. Together, they can work on options which may include the person having a conversation with their manager about changing their role to a more appropriate level. It could also include exploring ways to upskill or growing as needed to remain in the role.

If the person doesn't speak up or access appropriate support, the impact is not only on the individual but might also be felt across the organisation, thereby affecting the people they are leading.

Eventually, the person may 'feel like a failure' and either be asked to leave or make that decision themself. The person may have had lots of potential, and may initially have brought enthusiasm and energy to the role. However, the gap between the rise in responsibility and their growth and development was too large to sustain. It's almost like they were 'set up to fail'.

If the person is not personally and professionally equipped for the role, they might:

➪ avoid making decisions

➪ make unwise decisions

➪ not treat those they lead very well

➪ not be able to handle complex situations

Also, if they lead at the level they are at, rather than the level they are required to be at for the role, then the whole organisation might be dragged down to the level the leader is at.

Again, this is where a supervisor or mentor can assist the person to identify where they may be in their own growth and development and to be able to clearly see what is actually going on.

Being aware is half the battle: with knowledge comes the ability to put things in place to grow and develop such as strategies to get the assistance they need to be able to do the role at the level required.

A different scenario can also occur. Sometimes the person's maturity, expertise or capacity is <u>above</u> the position they are in.

When this happens, the person may:

➡ try to lead at a level higher than the role demands

➡ clash with other leaders because they don't remain at their designated level/operate within their job description

➡ lead at the level required of the role however they become bored and underchallenged

Having a supervisor or mentor to discuss and work on this can be really helpful.

We can find our own sweet spot where we get this balance just right. This is then an exciting place to live, room for growth but we are set up to win.

It also encourages people to live authentically, to be able to bring their whole self with just the appropriate amount of persona that is appropriate for the role.

This is much less exhausting and lessens the risk of the person burning out or simply walking away due to too much stress or pressure.

Being in the right role for the person is also a very important part of this, you can read about this in the chapter on being connected to your calling.

Ideally the person is in a role that has the right amount of challenge and opportunity to grow but not too much that it sets the person up to fail.

Supervision and mentoring can assist people to develop a plan to grow and develop both personally and professionally.

In the context of supervision, part of the initial contracting is to work together to set personal and professional development goals - to establish where the person is currently, where they want to be and what specific areas they need to grow and develop in.

Some of this work is about establishing what they need to learn. They may need to undertake some training or attend a professional development workshop in an area they would like to learn about or grow in.

They can also learn skills in a supervision session. The supervisee brings case studies or situations to reflect on and the process of supervision assists them to grow in the areas they have identified.

As the supervisor, you facilitate this learning and may be able to offer specific teaching if you are more experienced in the area that they want to learn about.

I have developed a simple diagram to help supervisors gain clarity about where a person is on their 'learning journey' in relation to a specific topic. I made the diagram because of the danger of the supervisor forgetting where the supervisee currently is in relation to their knowledge on that topic.

The Learning Journey

As supervisors, we might find ourselves just wanting to *tell* the supervisee what they 'need to do' and what they 'need to know' and expect that *like magic*, they will suddenly have all the knowledge and experience they need on a particular topic.

THE LEARNING JOURNEY DIAGRAM

|---|

Where they are   Where you are
(supervisee)   *(supervisor)*

In the learning journey diagram, the supervisor sits at a certain point along the line. They have worked their way, over time, to get where they are. They have done this by going through their own process of learning.

The supervisee sits at a different point on the line. This point is an indication of where they currently are in *their* learning journey.

If, as the supervisor, we simply drag the supervisee up to the point on the line where we are, the supervisee *will not be ready for it*. They are not ready because they have not gone through the process of learning for themselves.

Instead, what we need to do is to meet the supervisee where they are at on the line. Once we join them there, we can walk alongside and allow them to go through their own process of learning.

This is one of the reasons just giving advice is often unhelpful. It's a bit like giving someone the answers to a maths test: they might have the 'right answers' but they have no idea why. Giving the answers is not equipping them to succeed the next time they are asked to solve similar maths problems.

Actually, by giving the answers rather than allowing them to work out how to solve the maths equations on their own, we may be 'setting them up to fail'.

Just as we have shown above in the example about the maths test, it is much better if we can help someone to gain skills and understanding *for themselves* on the topic they are learning about. By doing so, we are empowering them to be able to work out the solution and know the steps to take. Otherwise, every time they have a new problem, they will be calling you for help.

Being called for help may actually feed into your need to be needed which can be unhealthy for you and for them.

Transformational Learning

The learning that someone engages in may be about 'what they do' but the other aspect of learning is about 'who they are'. This is the point where *transformational learning* comes in – when the learning is about 'who they are'.

As the person grows and develops, who they are changes. They are not just the same person with new skills added on - they are actually being transformed, as they learn, into the person that they 'need to be' for all that they 'want to do'.

Transformational learning happens as a person goes through the learning process themselves, growing and changing step by step.

Some learning takes time, some can happen quickly, especially when they have an aha moment and they see things differently.

Transformation occurs when we assimilate new information into the way we see or experience the world and our worldview expands and changes. Supervision is a great place for this to happen.

It can be a bit unsettling to consider a new way of thinking or to consider that things may not actually be the way you had always assumed they were. Sometimes it seems too much for us and we simply reject the new information, as it threatens our ability to feel safe in the world.

It takes courage to consider **new perspectives**. Having a safe place, one where we don't feel judged, provides an environment in which people can take risks with someone they trust.

In supervision, we put in place appropriate boundaries so as to not take advantage of a person who is in this potentially vulnerable position. What a privilege it is to journey alongside someone who is pushing the boundaries and challenging assumptions! It really becomes a sacred space: seeing someone being transformed, growing and developing both personally and professionally.

There are a number of activities, tools and resources throughout this book that can assist with personal and professional growth and development.

I encourage you to keep growing and developing new perspectives.

CHAPTER EIGHT

EMOTIONS AND BOUNDARIES

Walking into the room
I can sense the atmosphere
Emotions flying around
Yours and mine
Needing validation
To be seen and heard

The emotional boundary
Keeps us safe
I feel your pain
It reminds me of mine
But I'm staying grounded
Here in the moment with you

Leaving my triggers for later
To reflect on and process
I notice my empathy return
My focus is you
Reflecting your feelings
Respecting your dignity

Emotional Zone and Emotional Boundaries

I have developed a model that helps us to be aware of what's happening when we are with someone. I call this model 'The Emotional Zone Model'. The emotional zone is like a bubble that we enter into where we both feel that we can be emotionally safe.

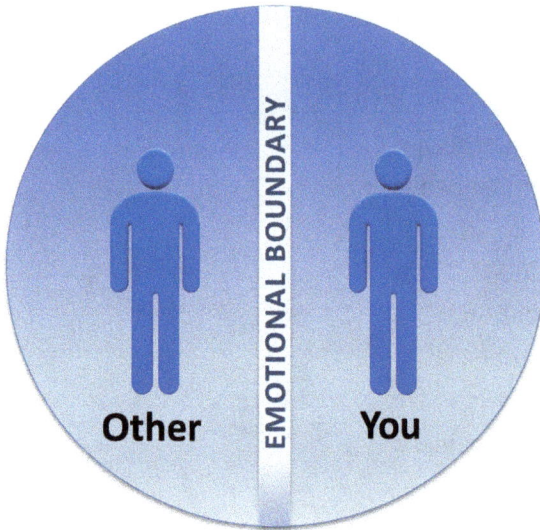

© Susan Marcuccio 2020

The emotional zone is the place where we make a connection with the other person. This is really our ultimate goal when we are having a meaningful interaction with someone:

*To enter into the emotional zone and be able to feel that we can communicate on a level that we **both** feel comfortable with.*

Before using the model, I recommend doing the following warmup activity: this is a great way to start thinking about our emotions and how we feel.

The activity helps us to remember a time when we felt happy and to be aware of the feelings evoked in us.

You can do this activity yourself or use it when you are working with someone who would like to have a greater awareness of how they are feeling and to be more aware of their emotional responses.

EMOTIONAL ZONE WARM UP ACTIVITY

1. Be aware of how you are feeling right now – name it.

2. Think of a positive experience when you felt happy.

3. Use your senses – how did it feel, smell, look, taste, sound?

4. Name the emotions – write them down.

Being able to be aware of our emotions is a very important part of self-reflection and is vital when we are providing support to others.

If we are *unaware* of how we are feeling, then it's less likely that we will notice when our *feelings change* or if we do notice, we may not be aware of *where* the feelings are coming from.

When two people enter the emotional zone, they both bring emotions with them that are then floating around in the 'emotional zone bubble'. I like to think of these emotions as little feeling words with wings that are flying around inside the bubble.

We can relate the 'flying emotions' to being like when you walk into a room and you can *sense the atmosphere*. It can be a joyful, happy atmosphere or a calm, peaceful atmosphere.

Sometimes when you walk into a room, you can get a sense that there is *something going on...* You may walk in and feel a sadness or some tension.

So, when you enter the emotional zone with someone, it can be very helpful to be aware of what the atmosphere is like. That is, to consider what <u>feeling words</u> are *flying around.*

Another important part of The Emotional Zone Model is the line down the middle: the emotional boundary. This line or boundary signifies the relationship that you have with the person.

The emotional boundary that you have with someone is very different depending on the role you have with that person. For example, the relationship you have with a family member is very different to a professional relationship.

Being aware of the emotional boundary is <u>key</u> to using The Emotional Zone Model. You can use the model with *any relationship and any role* but we will be exploring the model here in relation to your <u>professional</u> role.

USING THE EMOTIONAL ZONE MODEL

The first step in using the model is to be aware of how you are feeling. It's actually important to gain this awareness <u>before</u> you enter the emotional zone. The reason for this is:

It helps you to notice when your feelings change...

If you know how you are feeling <u>before</u> you enter the emotional zone, you at least know what you are about to take into the zone with you. The benefit of this is that you have an awareness of <u>your half</u> of the little feeling words that are flying around the zone (*mixing with the other person's little feeling words*).

Preparing to Enter The Emotional Zone

⬦ THE EMOTIONAL ZONE

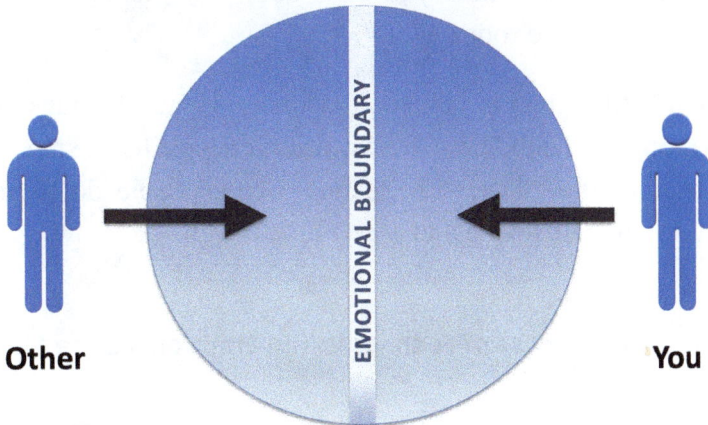

Other

EMOTIONAL BOUNDARY

You

© Susan Marcuccio 2020

As you prepare to enter the emotional zone (as shown by the two arrows), make sure you are clear in your own mind what your role is in relation to the other person. Also clarify that the other person is clear on your role for this interaction.

*You may have multiple roles in relation to the person, therefore, you need to be clear **upfront** about your role during this interaction. If you are functioning out of **more than one role** while in the emotional zone, it might be unclear where the emotional boundary is.*

It's important to make entering the emotional zone as inviting as you can whilst staying in your professional role. As you do so, take steps to let the other person knows there is a healthy emotional boundary in place.

Once the role is clear and the boundaries established, the person will hopefully feel comfortable to enter the emotional zone with you.

The other person will be bringing their own feelings into the emotional zone. So, now you have both <u>yours</u> and <u>their</u> feelings swirling around the room.

Wouldn't it be great if you could actually see the feelings? I have often thought it would be so much easier if people had a sign on their head stating how they were feeling. Some people do wear their emotions on their sleeve, but others hide it well.

Awareness of Feelings in The Emotional Zone

THE EMOTIONAL ZONE

Other's Feelings

Overwhelmed

Sad

Hopeless

Angry

Afraid

Frustrated

Hurt

EMOTIONAL BOUNDARY

Your Feelings

Confident

Happy

Hopeful

Peaceful

Calm

© Susan Marcuccio 2020

198

Once you have both entered the emotional zone, see if you can sense what emotions the *other person* has brought in. Notice if you start to feel different from when *you* came in.

For example, maybe you were feeling great when you came in: happy, peaceful, calm... But then you noticed that you were starting to feel a bit overwhelmed and sad. If *you* didn't bring these emotions in, then maybe they came in with the *other person*.

Each person enters the emotional zone with their own feelings. The feelings then swirl around the zone.

You can stay in your own feelings and change the atmosphere to be peaceful, calming and hopeful. You might also notice and start to feel the feelings of the other person (known as *transference*).

Transference of emotions can inform you of how the other person may be feeling <u>without</u> you taking the feelings on *as your own*. This is when you can move to advanced empathy.

Advanced Empathy

Advanced empathy is when you intuitively get a sense of what the other person may be feeling without them actually telling you. This can come by you noticing when your feelings change, and you notice a change in the atmosphere.

If the feelings are not coming from you, then they may be coming from the other person. If we are not aware of how we were feeling when we came in, then it's harder to pick this up.

Noticing these new emotions gives you an idea of what the other person may be feeling. This can be really helpful as it gives you information about what the other person might be experiencing, and this can help us to be a support to them. You can call this 'transference of feelings'. Their feelings transfer to you but you don't take them on as your own – they simply inform you. This is when you can reflect the feelings that they have back to them.

Reflecting Feelings

A communication skill that helps a person to feel noticed and heard is reflecting feelings. This is when you:

⇨ are told by the person how they are feeling and you reflect the feeling/s back to the person

or

⇨ you use advanced empathy to get a sense of what they are feeling without them actually telling you, then you reflect the feeling/s back to the person

For example, you may say to the person:

⇨ "I'm noticing some sadness in your voice."
⇨ "You seem a bit frustrated about that."

This helps the person to feel validated.

Validation

When a person is feeling a certain way, they can feel very supported if someone validates their feelings. This might occur if:

⇨ they tell you how they are feeling and they feel <u>heard</u> by you

or

⇨ you sense they are feeling something and reflect that feeling <u>back to them</u>

A person can feel so supported when someone acknowledges that they are feeling a certain feeling. The reality is that it's not really about whether the person is feeling a 'right' or 'wrong' emotion: it's about the fact that they are feeling that <u>particular</u> emotion.

When someone has a feeling acknowledged in a supportive way, we call that *validation*. Once their feeling has been validated, they can often let the feeling go, especially if it's a feeling that they <u>don't want</u> to feel.

Having a feeling *validated* can also bring the intensity of the emotion down. This occurs because:

➪ the person feels heard by you in relation to the feeling

➪ they no longer have to convince you that they have that particular feeling

➪ they don't feel a need to increase the intensity of the emotion to try to justify that the feeling they have is valid

In summary, to recognise and manage transference:

➪ Know how you feel before you enter the emotional zone
➪ Notice when your feelings change – name the feeling/s
➪ Recognise that the change in your own feelings is a clue to what the other person is feeling
➪ Recognise that what is occurring is *transference* of the client's feelings (and <u>not</u> your own feelings)
➪ Respond to the client as appropriate, with advanced empathy, reflecting feelings, validating and being fully present with them

Recognising and Managing Triggers

Sometimes when you start to feel a feeling that is coming from the other person, you identify with that feeling. In other words, you remember feeling that feeling yourself. As you remember, you are reminded of a time (or times) when you felt that same way. This experience is what we call a 'trigger', as it triggers a memory or a feeling that you have had before.

We can all experience triggers when we are with someone. It can be very helpful to be aware of these triggers and to know how we can respond when we are triggered.

Being triggered may cause us to have a reaction because of the reminders of the previous event or experience. We sometimes remember the feelings we had (during the event or experience) more than the actual details of the event.

If it was a positive experience, being triggered can cause us to remember and feel the positive feelings we had such as joy, excitement and contentment.

If we are triggered by a negative or traumatic experience, we might remember and feel the negative feelings we had at the time such as fear, anger or being overwhelmed.

We can be triggered by:

➪ being in the presence of someone

➪ thinking about being with a particular person

➪ remembering (or anticipating) an event

➪ hearing a story or a noise

➪ seeing a person or image

➩ watching a movie or clip

➩ having someone or something touch us

➩ smelling or tasting something that we associate with an event or experience

➩ many other things

Sometimes the memory of an experience can almost transports us to another place, and we are no longer mentally present.

If we are triggered, then what can we do to keep ourselves or those we are supporting safe?

A grounding exercise can help us to get back into the present (which we might call the *here and now*) and therefore, back to a 'safe place'.

GROUNDING EXERCISE

Here is the simple grounding exercise I use:

1. Sit on a chair
2. Put your feet on ground
3. Feel your feet making contact with the floor
4. Notice where your body is making contact with the chair
5. Look around the room and notice three objects
6. Name the three objects that you can see
7. You can say the names out loud (or say them in your head)

This simple grounding exercise is effective in helping you to be present in (or come back to) the room rather than being 'caught up in the memory' of a previous event.

You might like to assist someone else to use the grounding exercise if you become aware that they have been triggered. However, it's important to recognise that you may need to refer a person to receive specialist assistance if they are being triggered: we must be careful to stay within the boundaries of our role and refer as required.

If *you* are triggered when you are in your professional role, you might like to try doing the grounding exercise discreetly. As mentioned, you can notice three objects in the room and name them without speaking out aloud.

It may not be appropriate to *stop and reflect in the moment* in order to process what's happening for you. If this is the case and you feel able to keep going with the session (and process the trigger later) then there is another exercise you can do:

Staying Present When You Are Triggered

THE EMOTIONAL ZONE

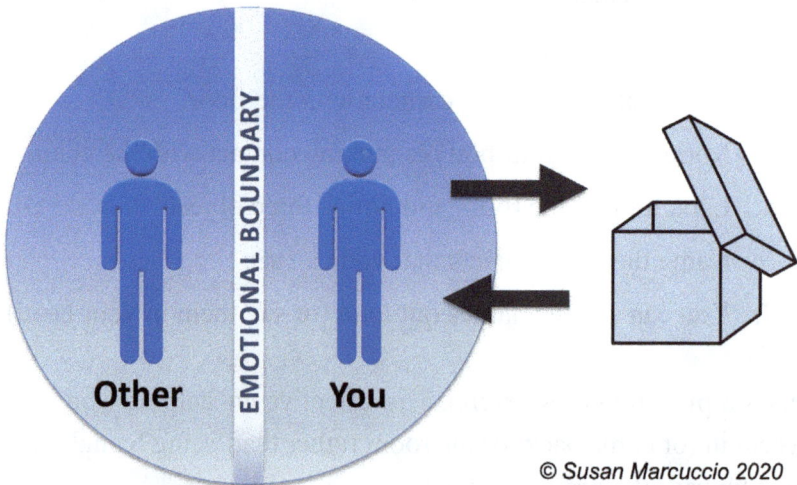

© Susan Marcuccio 2020

In order to stay present in the emotional zone, imagine you are capturing the trigger with your hand and placing it outside the emotional zone (as shown by the top arrow in the diagram). Leave the trigger there (in your box of emotions) to process later. Then, come back into the emotional zone (as shown by the bottom arrow) and be present with the other person.

You must remember after you have finished with the person to pick the trigger back up (that is, go back and get the 'trigger' that you placed in your box of emotions).

At that point, you can:

➡ reflect on what happened to you in the emotional zone and do what you need to do to process the trigger
➡ plan for a future time to process the trigger on your own
➡ identify that you may need to process the trigger with another person like a supervisor

*In rare cases, it may not be enough to put the trigger outside the emotional zone (and into your box of emotions). Instead, you may feel that the trigger is **so overwhelming** that you need to leave the emotional zone (and the interaction with person you were supporting) and **not go back in.***

If this happens, <u>and</u> you feel unable to continue with the interaction, take the necessary steps needed to ensure the other person is safe, remove yourself from the situation and get immediate professional support.

Recognising and Managing Countertransference

When we are triggered, it can take us into *countertransference*. This is when the feelings that we noticed in the other person transfer onto us, we are triggered and then we start to lose our own feelings that we had when we came into the emotional zone. We *feel the feelings* from the <u>other person</u> however, rather than just letting it inform us about what is happening for the other person (transference), the feelings <u>become ours</u>. When we take on the feelings as our own, this is no longer just transference. Now – this is *countertransference*.

For example, the person you are supporting may be feeling sad. You were aware at the start of the session that you felt happy and you entered the emotional zone in a happy state. But at some point into the session:

*You started to feel the feelings of **sadness**.*

THE EMOTIONAL ZONE

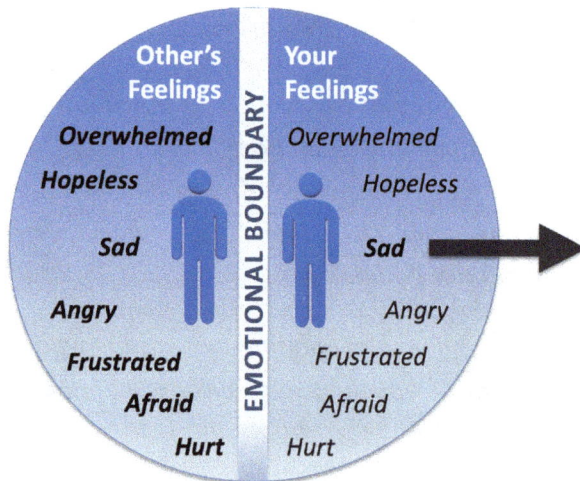

© Susan Marcuccio 2020

We can see from this diagram that the feelings of the other person are now also on your side of the emotional zone. The <u>other person's</u> feelings have become <u>your</u> feelings. You are now experiencing *countertransference. (Note that you may take on just one or a few of their feelings rather than all of them.)*

Once you start to experience countertransference, it's unlikely that you can be present in the moment and be a support to the other person as you are probably using <u>most if not all of your energy</u> to keep yourself safe and okay. In other words, you may find yourself 'leaving the emotional zone' (as represented by the arrow).

If you get caught in countertransference, you may not notice it until you reflect on it after the session. In other words, you later realise that you 'stayed in' the session but were not really present 'emotionally'.

If you realise that you took on the feelings of the person you were supporting, acknowledge what happened and – *learn from it.* Make a note to be more aware next time, especially if you notice your feelings start to change. *It's okay to experience and acknowledge countertransference: it's how we learn and – it happens to us all!*

Empathy as an Indicator

Lack of empathy for the person you are with is a good indicator that you have been triggered or are experiencing countertransference. This might be happening because you still need to *process* a situation or you need to do *more processing.*

When you are triggered or are experiencing countertransference, you are less able to be present with the other person. That means you are less able to consider what is going on *for them* as your focus has become about *your own feelings.*

Once you reflect and realise what is happening *for you*, it's usually possible to put your focus back on the client, including having *empathy for them.*

If you are triggered by someone, for example: a colleague, you may become angry with that person. You might feel frustrated, fearful or hurt. You may feel you can't forgive the person for what has happened, based on something they have (or haven't) done.

Even though you may hide these emotions, it's quite possible the other person senses how you are feeling. They may realise that you don't seem to have empathy or compassion for them even though it's what they would expect from you in the current situation.

A good indicator that you have processed the trigger or have been able to put it aside to work on later, is when you start to feel empathy and compassion for the person.

You may not ever agree with what they have done or not done (which is okay), but you have 'removed the arrow from your heart' and now have the clarity you need to view the situation more objectively.

Box of Emotions

I find when people come to supervision for the first time, and they haven't engaged in any personal work or counselling, they present with lots of unprocessed emotions.

I use the analogy of a **box of emotions:**

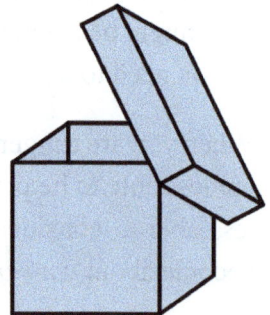

Every time they *engage in conversation or support someone* in their professional role, and they have to put aside their own emotions, they 'stuff the emotions' in the box. If this keeps happening and they never go back to the emotions that they have put in the box to process them, this results in a:

Very full box!

Every time you experience an emotion that you can't or don't process straight away, you put it in your box of emotions. Over time, this builds up and then eventually you try and put **one more emotion** in the box and the whole box **explodes!!** As all the emotions spill out:

It can be messy...

We need to find a safe place to remove the lid, take the emotions out the box and *process each one*. We may want to do this with a supervisor, mentor or chaplain or see someone else in a suitable role, such as a counsellor or psychologist.

How to Process the Triggers, Countertransference and Emotions

Once we have opened our box of emotions, we can take the unprocessed items out and work with them. As supervisors, we don't take the lid off the supervisee's emotional box: we allow the *person* to take the lid off and bring out something they want to work on, when *they feel ready.*

A person can process something by taking the time to reflect on it. For example, they may be feeling angry about a situation and they have stuffed *anger* in the box. While it is unprocessed, it just festers. The person may decide to bring it to supervision and to spend time reflecting on the situation that caused them to feel angry.

By looking at the situation, gaining new perspectives, being able to share it with someone, feeling heard and have the feelings validated, they may no longer feel angry. The *anger* (associated with this situation) is now no longer sitting in the box of emotions.

If the *anger* still needs *more processing,* or some action needs to be taken, it may still be in the box, but part of the processing has been done.

Sometimes it takes a while to process some of the emotions associated with the triggers that have been put in the box, but gradually, as a person works through the contents of their box:

The box gets lighter!

Emotions can also be processed by journaling or taking time to get away to spend in reflection. It can be as simple as *writing it down* and then *tearing up the piece of paper* or something else symbolic.

Many of the reflective exercises that we do in supervision can assist with this work of processing emotions.

Getting Triggered Out of The Emotional Zone

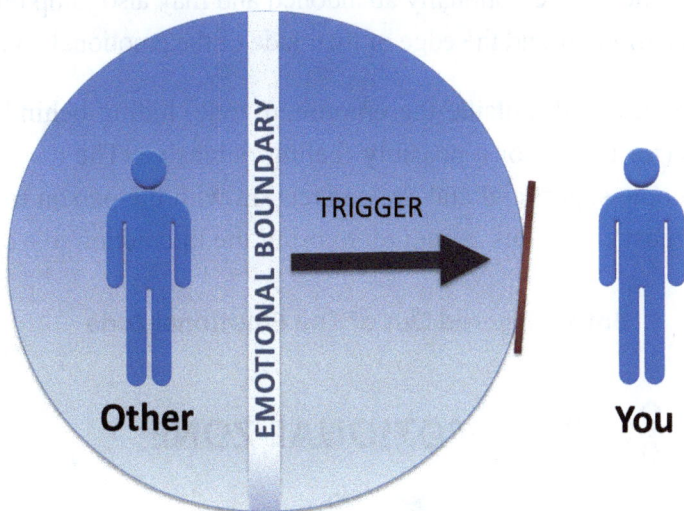

© Susan Marcuccio 2020

Imagine for a moment that you are now in the emotional zone with the person that you are supporting, and you have been triggered and have moved into countertransference. You are not aware of what's going on, but you suddenly feel unsafe, and you jump out of the emotional zone.

You then put up a barrier around the edge of the emotional zone to keep yourself safe and you stay out of the emotional zone. This is represented by the red line on the diagram, showing that there is now a barrier that is stopping you returning back into the emotional zone.

At this point, you may be able to *physically stay* with the person but you are no longer *present emotionally* (because you have jumped out of the emotional zone). The person you are supporting may sense that you have jumped out and are no longer present *with them*.

They can then feel emotionally abandoned and may also jump out and put up a barrier around the edge of their side of the emotional zone.

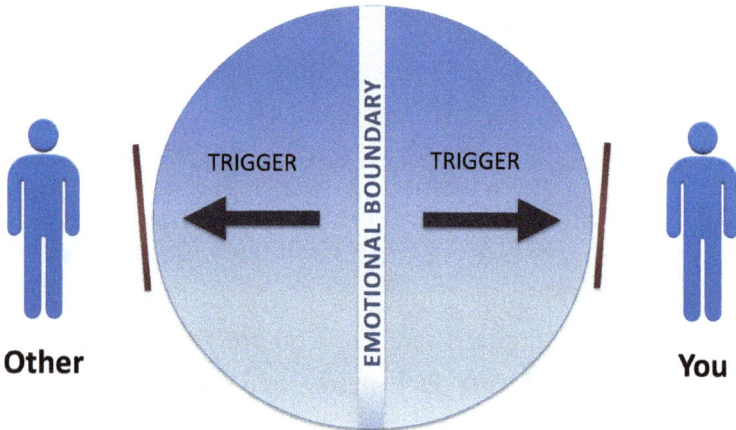

Now you are both outside the emotional zone, hiding behind your barriers (for protection), possibly feeling defensive. The discussion may become superficial and the connection with the person may be lost. In most cases, this is enough to bring the interaction to a close.

Both Triggered Out of The Emotional Zone

THE EMOTIONAL ZONE

TRIGGER   EMOTIONAL BOUNDARY   TRIGGER

Other   You

© Susan Marcuccio 2020

NB: Sometimes the situation <u>is unsafe</u> and the trigger works as a **warning** for us to get to safety.

If you are still in the emotional zone and the other person gets triggered and jumps out, the temptation is to cross the emotional boundary to reach them and to try and bring them back into the emotional zone.

Warning: There are consequences for crossing the emotional boundary (as shown by the red flashing light) which can include finding it difficult to remain in your professional role and it becoming unsafe for the other person and for you.

When You Cross the Emotional Boundary

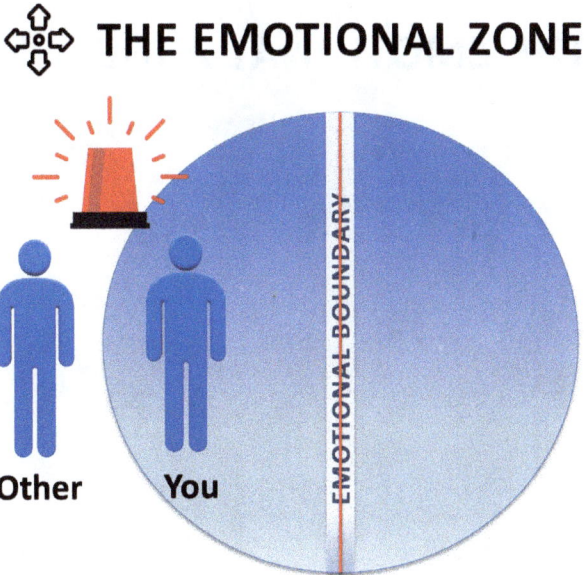

THE EMOTIONAL ZONE

Other You

EMOTIONAL BOUNDARY

© Susan Marcuccio 2020

Rather than crossing the emotional boundary, try to stay calm and stay in your side of the emotional zone. If you manage to do that, the person may decide to come back in.

Another situation that can occur is if the other person doesn't respect your professional role and tries to become too familiar. They may then try and cross the emotional boundary to get closer to you.

Warning: There are consequences for allowing the other person to cross the emotional boundary (as shown by the red flashing light) which can include finding it difficult to remain in your professional role and it becoming unsafe for the other person and for you.

When They Cross the Emotional Boundary

THE EMOTIONAL ZONE

EMOTIONAL BOUNDARY

Other You

© Susan Marcuccio 2020

It is important that we stay in our professional role and keep a strong boundary in place, for their sake and for ours.

The ideal is that we are both in the emotional zone, not crossing the emotional boundary but staying on our own side, feeling emotionally safe so we can communicate well.

© Susan Marcuccio 2020

Emotional Zone Summary:

➡ Be clear on the role you have with the person - establish a healthy emotional boundary.

➡ Know how you are feeling before you enter the emotional zone - name the feelings.

➡ As you step into the emotional zone, be aware of the feelings you are bringing in.

➪ Invite the person into the emotional zone, establish an emotionally healthy space.

➪ Be aware of the atmosphere in the room and the emotions swirling around.

➪ Notice if your feelings change and let it inform you what the person may be feeling.

➪ Use advanced empathy, validation and reflecting of feelings so the person feels heard.

➪ If you get triggered, then recognise it and capture it and place it outside the zone.

➪ Come back into the emotional zone and be fully present with the person.

➪ Keep checking that you don't cross over the emotional boundary.

➪ If they are triggered out of the emotional zone, stay present and calm.

➪ If the person decides to come back in, keep supporting them.

➪ If they decide to stay out, let them go but follow up (as appropriate).

➪ Notice what emotions you take out of the emotional zone.

➪ If your feelings are different to what you brought in - they may need to be processed.

➪ Make sure you make time to process your emotions, triggers and countertransference.

➪ Regularly see your supervisor to ensure that you are staying emotionally healthy.

Boundaried Spaces

Sometimes when people come to supervision, they are feeling very overwhelmed and unable to process all that is happening in their lives. Everything seems to be enmeshed and they just cannot get clarity. Being able to separate out the different areas into boundaried spaces can assist the person to start to feel calmer, gain perspective and see more clearly the way forward.

⬖ Boundaried Spaces

© Susan Marcuccio 2020

Here is how I developed this tool:

A supervisee came to a session very distraught; she had a conflict between a work event and a family gathering. Unable to decide what to do and which one to go to, she had decided to *try and do both*. Her stress levels were 'through the roof' and she was not enjoying the lead up to either event as she could not work out how to be present at both places.

I must admit, I felt a bit overwhelmed just hearing her story and dilemma, and I had to try and not over identify with her situation, as I too had found myself in a *similar situation* many times. When I asked her what she wanted to get from supervision on this day, she said she wanted to work on how to be *fully present* in each space.

As I thought about the best way for us to work together in the reflective space, an activity came into my mind. I could see two separate spaces - I called them **boundaried spaces**.

So, we moved into the reflective space, and I asked her to draw two boxes and to dedicate each box to each event. She chose the situation that she wanted to look at first. This was her family 'boundaried space'. She was then able to add everything into that box that was important to her, specifically looking at her hopes for the family event.

I noticed a shift in her posture and her countenance: she started smiling and getting excited, and I felt such a change in her. I mentioned that she seemed a bit different, and she said:

"Yes, I'm so happy that I can now focus on this family event - it's going to be such a special time..."

As we reflected on her responsibilities for getting everything ready for the family event, she realised that she could complete the preparations the day before. That meant she only needed to arrive at the same time as other guests, thus freeing up time beforehand to go to the other event first.

I then asked her to look at the second box, her work 'boundaried space'. She added in everything that was meaningful to her about the work event and again her face lit up.

"It's going to be amazing," she said. "I just can't believe I still get to be part of this special work event..."

After spending time together considering her commitments at the work event, she realised she could delegate many of the tasks to lighten her load. That meant she was still involved but not overloaded, so had time to enjoy both events.

After she had spent time on each boundaried space, I asked her what it was like to do that activity and what she had noticed. She spoke about the realisation that each boundaried space was so special and the joy she received by being able to go into each one and to have a boundary around it.

She then went on to say that she now saw how she could do both by making a few adjustments. She would go to the work event <u>first</u> - keeping the boundaried space. While she was there, she would be fully present with her colleagues and the many visitors she was expecting. She could then move on to the family event and keep in the boundaried space while she was there, in order to be fully present with her family.

When she had arrived, both events were enmeshed and she couldn't see a way forward. By doing this simple activity, she had her joy back. *'Boundaries Spaces' then became another activity in my toolbox - one that I have used many times.*

BOUNDARIED SPACES ACTIVITY:

Step One: Write down all the events that are coming up.

Step Two: Take a blank piece of paper and add only the events to the page that are really important to you.

Step Three: Draw a box around each event to make the boundaried spaces.

Step Four: Add any other events that you can't or don't want to say no to and make boundaried spaces for those too (so each event has a box around it).

Step Five: Now look at what you have on the page and see what you notice about the boundaried spaces that you have added.

Step Six: Work on each of the boundaried spaces individually so you have a plan for each one. Debrief from one space before going onto the next and don't let anything from the previous event make its way into the boundaried space that you are working on.

Step Seven: Now look at the boundaried spaces all together to see what is needed to go forward.

This activity usually helps the person to work with each boundaried space individually before viewing them all together. Otherwise, it can all seem to be enmeshed and overwhelming and it's hard for the person to gain clarity. Maybe try it for yourself and see if you find it helpful!

CHAPTER NINE

REFLECTIVE PRACTICE

It takes courage
To stop and look back
To look deeper
To ponder
To wonder
To look beneath

It takes curiosity
To wonder why
To take another look
To ask questions
To consider
To reflect

It takes creativity
To see it another way
To gain clarity
To see differently
To be transformed
To see new perspectives

What is Reflective Practice?

There are many different definitions of the term *reflective practice*. My definition of reflective practice is when a person takes the time to stop and reflect about their work, their profession, a situation, a case, a scenario, really anything they would like to look at, in order to learn from it. We can interchange other words with 'reflect' – we can use: 'think about', 'ponder' or 'consider'.

A *reflective practice* is something that a person can put in place and do on a regular basis or even include as part of their usual routine. It's something that people can do on their own through methods like journaling or using their own activities to help them reflect.

Really anyone can engage in reflective practice, but people often find it easier to reflect with someone else: supervision is designed to assist people in this practice. Supervisors are trained to guide people through the reflective practice process. Reflective practice assists people to gain perspective and have greater clarity about specific situations and also their life in general, enabling them to learn from their experiences.

Engaging in Reflective Practice

A helpful way of engaging in reflective practice is to use reflective or creative models, tools and resources. In supervision, there is usually an opportunity to do this once you get to the reflective stage of the process of supervision. It's not always easy to move into the reflective space, so having an activity to help engage in reflective practice can assist both the supervisor and the supervisee.

Taking time to engage with the activity tends to slow the process down and really helps the supervisee see the situation they are bringing to supervision from a different perspective.

I use the Perspective Supervision Process Model (explained in Chapter Four): once I have listened to the person and we have contracted for the session, we work together to get a focus. Then we move to the *reflective space*.

Once we are in the reflective space, this is where we decide together how are we going to reflect on this situation. I usually consider which tool may be the most appropriate one for what the person is hoping to get from supervision on that day. I then suggest a way that we could work with it or suggest a couple of options for them to choose from.

Creative Supervision

Here is an example of a creative way to engage in reflective practice, using a simple drawing tool:

DRAW YOUR SITUATION TOOL

One tool I find quite easy to use both face to face and online is for the supervisee to do a simple drawing of the situation that they have brought to supervision. I ask the following types of questions as I guide the supervisee through using the tool:

1. "If you had to describe your situation without words, what would you draw?"

This is to get them thinking about the situation in a different way. If it is face to face, I usually have white A4 paper, a clip board, a pen and coloured markers available. If it's online, I ask the person to get a piece of paper and a pen.

2. *"Go ahead and draw your situation, using a pen, pencils or coloured markers."*

Encourage them to not 'over think' it, but to just put on the paper what comes to mind. There is no right or wrong and it doesn't matter if they think they are not a good drawer. It can be a literal drawing, an image, a symbol or even a 'colour' that represents different aspects of the scenario.

3. *"Have a look at what you have drawn and see if you would like to add anything?"*

Most people, when they are encouraged to have another look, add something to their picture. This is part of the reflective process - having another look.

Don't try and analyse what they have drawn, just affirm them for having a go at something different.

4. *"What are you noticing as you look at your picture?"*

Allow them to show you and tell you about their picture. Again, don't try and analyse the picture or share what the picture means to you.

If it seems appropriate, you *may* want to offer something you have observed about the picture such as the position of the people or any key features that you notice.

For some people, going this far with the tool is enough. They are able to gain insight and perspective just by drawing the scenario.

If the supervisee has benefited from using the tool, it's suitable to stop at the end of step four. However, you may like to continue on through further steps for some supervisees.

If the situation seems to call for it, continue on with these additional steps:

5. *"Would you like to add some words to your picture?"*

This gives your supervisee the opportunity to add some descriptive words that may help to broaden the perspective or give clarity to the situation.

Explain that they can write individual words or short phrases (as many or as few as they like). Some people might write full sentences which is also okay.

6. *"As you look at your picture now, what are you noticing?"*

This gives them another opportunity to ponder and reflect on their situation by seeing it before them on a piece of paper (rather than just thinking about it in their head) and also read the words that have been added.

It is amazing what can emerge at this point...

Again, you can offer observations but don't try and tell them what you think it means:

Let them do that!

If it is pastoral supervision, and the person has already said they would like to reflect *theologically* on what they bring to supervision, I may ask this additional question:

6.a *"As you look at your paper, I wonder where God is in this picture?"*

They may reflect on this for a while and then add where they think God is. This can bring wonderful insight for people, and it can also be very comforting.

Be aware that at times, asking this question can also be confronting. It does however often bring a deeper level of understanding for the person so can be a very helpful exercise to undertake.

Going as far as question 6 (or 6.a) may be enough for the person. Sometimes I notice that the person still seems a bit stuck in their situation, and I will continue on with even further questions:

7. *"Now on a new piece of paper, can you draw the situation again the way you would like it to be."*

This allows them to now imagine the scenario differently and helps them to unveil how they would actually like the situation to be. It can be amazing to see the different version and for the person to see it another way.

We would then repeat the steps of the activity (as above), asking them to reflect (step 4) and possibly add words (step 5), particularly if they have added words to the first picture. Ask them what they are noticing (step 6.) You could also as them where God is (step 6.a) if you had asked that in the first picture.

Once they have both pictures finished, I would continue on to the following questions:

8. "As you look at the two pictures, what do you notice? What are the similarities and differences that you are seeing?"

This allows them to clearly articulate what they see when comparing the two pictures. The similarities show what is already *as they would like it to be*, and the differences show the changes *they would like to happen.*

9. "What will it take for you to get from the first picture to the second picture?"

This then starts to move the situation from reflection to action. The question is an invitation to start thinking about the different options they might have.

I sometimes add another step:

10. "You may like to draw one final picture that sits between the two you have already drawn: a picture that joins the two together and show what needs to happen."

This step enables the supervisee to use the activity of drawing as they work through the *action stage*. This can sometimes unlock ideas that they couldn't previously see.

I finish up the drawing tool with some final questions. Use these questions at whatever point you finish the activity with the supervisee (step 4, 6, 9 or 10).

Final Questions:

➪ *"As we finish this reflective activity today, what are you going to take with you from the reflective space?"*

➪ *"What new perspectives have been revealed?"*

➪ *"What might this mean for you now?"*

These questions allow the person to mention the key learning and fresh thinking that has come from being in the reflective space and engaging in this activity. It also brings the activity to a close.

We would then move to the *review stage* of the Perspective Supervision Process Model, and I would then ask them what it was like to engage in that activity.

Other Resources for Reflection

You can also use other ways to reflect in supervision and mentoring such as:

➪ Picture cards

➪ Using shapes

➪ Using objects

➪ Metaphors

Picture Cards

There are many creative ways to use picture cards both in face to face and online supervision sessions. One way I use them is to invite the supervisee to choose two sets of cards from a pile of cards that I hand them to look through (or I hold up, if online).

➡ The first set of cards represents the *current situation* they are in

➡ The second set of cards represents *how they would like the situation to be*

NB: I suggest the supervisee chooses two or three cards per set.

First Set of Cards

We start working with the first set of cards (*the current situation*). While we are doing this, the second set of cards are put to the side, face down.

STEP 1: I invite them to choose the card they would like to start with and ask what it was that <u>drew them</u> to that particular card.

The other cards in the first set are face down at this point so we are only looking at one card at a time.

STEP 2: Once they have told me what it was about that card that they were drawn to, I ask them to look at the picture again.

I do this to get them to see if there is anything else that they didn't see the first time.

STEP 3: I then invite them to look <u>a third time</u> in case there's anything they missed that they would now like to talk about.

STEP 4: Once they have looked at each card from the first set individually, I invite them to place these cards out in front of them, all at the same time, in order to look at them together (or if online, I hold all the cards up at the same time).

STEP 5: I then ask them to look for any similarities or differences amongst the cards.

STEP 6: I also ask them to talk about 'what it's like' to look at all the cards together and to share what they notice.

I don't give my opinion about their card choices or analyse what they have said. I might offer something that I have noticed (that they haven't mentioned) if I think it would be helpful.

Second Set of Cards

We then repeat Steps 1 to 6 using the second set of cards (the cards for *how they would like the situation to be).*

Once they finish Step 6 (looking at all the cards together with the set), I ask them to move onto some further steps:

STEP 7: I ask the supervisee to put the first set of cards in front of them (or I hold them up if online) whilst still looking at the second set. At this point, they have up to six cards in front of them (the two combined sets).

STEP 8: I then ask them to reflect on the <u>differences</u> between the first set of cards (*the situation now)* and the second set of cards (how they would *like it to be).*

STEP 9: Finally, we discuss together: "What is it going to take to get from where you are now to where you want to be?"

Often the answer has become clearer during the exercise.

Using Shapes

Another reflective tool I use is to ask the person to map out the scenario on a piece of paper by adding shapes to their page:

"Draw a shape for each person or each part of the scenario that is in this situation."

Once they have done that, I ask them about the shapes they have drawn:

"Tell me about each shape and what it represents."

This is a way of getting the person out of the story and to see new perspectives as they reflect on the bigger picture. It can be very helpful for them to realise which shape they have allocated to each person or part of the scenario. This often reveals some really interesting results.

Again, don't try and analyse but just use it as a reflective activity to get the person to see the situation differently.

This activity could also be undertaken by offering the person plastic or wooden shapes to choose from. The shapes could be placed onto the table or floor or even a magnetic board.

Using Objects

You can also have a bag or box of objects that the person can choose from to represent the people or parts of a situation. For example, you could have a box which contains figurines, toy animals, different size rocks, pencils, pieces of wool/string, fluffy objects and harsh objects (such as a piece of metal).

Feel free to use your imagination to include a range of items in your bag or box: most small objects are suitable for this activity.

If online, you can ask the person to choose some objects from around their own room. For example, a cup, a plant, a bag or a stapler (or other stationery items). This gives the person something tangible to look at, hold and feel. Using the senses this way with concrete items helps them to 'see it differently' – often with more clarity.

You can ask them to tell you about each object and why they chose it. You can also ask them to put the objects on the table to map out the scenario. It is quite interesting then to see where they put each object in relation to the other objects and to see the different size or other distinctive aspects of each object.

It's quite amazing to see what emerges by using these creative tools. Don't try and analyse or do the work for them. Allow the person to do their own reflection whilst you simply accompany them.

Metaphors

Metaphors are a powerful tool to use in supervision and mentoring. You can either *listen out* for metaphors the person might use, such as:

It felt like…

➡ wading through mud
➡ carrying a heavy load
➡ paddling under the water

You can then use the metaphor by inviting them to stop and reflect on what that metaphor *means to them*.

If they haven't offered a metaphor, you can ask them for one and see what they come up with. You can then use their metaphor as the basis for their reflection on the situation they have brought.

This 'mental picture' that they share can be very meaningful and often the person can elaborate on the metaphor which can be very revealing for them.

Many of these creative reflective tools such as picture cards, shapes, objects and metaphors, can also be used in *creative group supervision* and you can see how to use them specifically in that context in the next chapter.

You may have other creative tools that you use, or you could create some of your own.

Anything that invites the person to look at something <u>concrete</u> *as a representation of their* <u>abstract thoughts</u>, *even if just for a moment, can help them to see* **new perspectives***!*

Having a Voice

I was working with a supervisee online during a COVID-19 lockdown. The supervisee expressed that he was unsure of what to 'bring to supervision' to talk about.

He went on to say that he was *unable to do his job* due to the current circumstances. I sensed that he had a lot to say but didn't know where to start as he didn't have a 'case' to bring.

I asked him if he would like to do a sort of 'check in', to see how he was going with his changed circumstances. That way, he could reflect on his current situation. He said that would be great.

I started to think of a way for us to work together to allow him to share what was going on for him without it being too confronting...

I decided to ask him to draw a picture of himself, saying it could simply be a stick figure or could be something a bit more elaborate.

As I talked about the steps with this person, I actually was 'thinking on my feet', that is, I was *designing a new tool* as I went along.

This 'creative' method of working with people seems to happen to me a lot. I find myself faced with an unencountered situation so:

I <u>develop</u> a new model, tool or resource!

Sometimes as I start to speak, I have no idea what I'm going to say. However, most often, it seems to work. I guess you could say:

"I trust the process of supervision to happen."

THE HAVING A VOICE TOOL

I have now used this activity, which I call the 'Having a Voice Tool' with many people. As I invite people to take part in the 'Having a Voice Tool', I always say: "There are no wrong answers! This is the opportunity for you to *have a voice* and for someone to *listen to you*!"

For many people, no one has ever asked them the sorts of questions that come up when using this tool. It's such a privilege to be in a position of asking things that no one has possibly ever asked before...

My supervisee listened to my suggestion and drew a picture of himself. I then asked him to add anything that would make the picture *uniquely* him. He then added something to his picture that was important to him.

When I ask people to add something to the picture, some have drawn: a person or a number of people. Some have included an object or something to do with their faith. Some have drawn something related to a hobby or their work, something they are passionate about or something which is meaningful to them.

As I continued to work with my supervisee and his drawing of himself, I asked him to write something next to the mouth on his picture:

"What do you want to say?"

He then wrote down what he wanted to say. Then I asked him:

"What do you want to hear?"

For this question, he drew two ears then wrote two answers, one next to each ear. The next question was:

"What do you want to see?"

Again, he wrote two answers near his two eyes. I added another question around the senses after I had used the activity a few times:

"What do you want to smell?"

This often has a profound answer. It's amazing how smell can transport us to a different place. He wrote one answer next to his nose. Then I asked:

"What do you want to think about?"

As I asked this last question, I pointed to the top of his head.

Some people tell me their answers as we go through the model and some wait until they've heard all the questions before sharing.

If they have been telling me their thoughts as we go, I find that around this point (the top of the head), I often notice themes emerging. I don't try and analyse what they share but simply validate them for sharing with me.

I may sometimes ask a question for clarification or invite the person to tell me more about a particular aspect if they would like to.

Next, as I used the 'Having a Voice Tool', I moved to the person's hands.

"What would you like to do?"

He gave two answers to match the two hands in his drawing. Then:

"Where would you like to go?"

Similarly, this resulted in two answers, one for each foot.

These last two questions allowed him to stop and consider what he would *like to do* and where he would *like to go*.

The answers to these questions vary so much from person to person. I always encourage people to not 'over think' their answers but to write down the first thing that comes into their mind...

It's fascinating to see what emerges.

Not over thinking takes away the danger of writing what they think they <u>should write</u> rather than what the person really <u>wants to say</u>.

The next question as I use this tool is:

"What's in your heart?"

We have spent time building up to this one and by now hopefully the person is feeling safe enough to reveal what's first and foremost the focus of their heart *right now*.

We are really now walking on 'sacred ground'. If you use this exercise, be so careful to be respectful and really hold the space. You don't know what the person will reveal.

This tool can be used in many contexts, the important thing is to stay in whatever role you are in with this person. Just listen, don't try and analyse or fix anything.

The gift is in giving the person the opportunity to have a voice and to know that you are someone that can simply be present with them as they share.

As I continued with the supervisee, he shared what was in his heart. I then deliberately asked the next question as I pointed to the top of my arms:

"Where do you get your strength from?"

Again, I asked him for two answers (one for each arm).

I ask this particular question as I find it helps to remind the person of where they draw their strength. This might be important after they have left the session with me, particularly if the activity has evoked some emotion.

I then asked him to tell me about the thing he had added to his picture and what prompted him to include it: what was meaningful for him about what he added; how did it help the picture to be uniquely about him?

Sharing something unique about themselves finishes the activity with a focus on something meaningful that can lift a person's spirit and starts to get them ready to leave the session in a good place. *This is important, as we don't want to invite a person to open up about* *their life at the moment and to **have a voice** and then just leave them in an open and vulnerable place.*

As we were moving to the *summary* part of the session, I asked my supervisee the following questions:

➪ "Now that you have completed this activity, what did you notice?"

➪ "What has emerged for you?"

➪ "Did you notice any themes?"

➪ "Did anything surprise you about what you wrote?"

➪ "What does this mean for you now?"

Asking these questions helps the person to learn more about themselves and gives them the opportunity to consider if they want to take any action as a result of any new perspectives.

To assist my supervisee to get back into the 'here and now', I asked him what it was like to do the exercise. This helped him to move into the final stage of the supervision process (*review)* before leaving the session.

Before finishing the session, we need to make sure that the person is back in the 'here and now', being able to access their coping mechanisms and back to cognitive thinking.

Let's think back to my supervisee when he first arrived that day. He hadn't known what to discuss because he was unable to do his job at that time. Doing this exercise with him seemed to really give him a voice and revealed to him where he was at that moment and what was important to him.

This is a great exercise to do with someone who arrives at supervision and feels like they don't have a 'case' to bring or anything to share. It gives them a vehicle to have a voice and then reflect on the findings.

The 'Having a Voice Tool' is very revealing to the person: of all the things they could have drawn and written on that day, in answer to the questions, they get to reflect on what they *actually wrote*.

I wonder how you would answer if you were asked these questions today?

This activity went so well with my supervisee on that day that I wrote it up in my book of models and tools and started using it as a 'go-to' tool in my toolkit.

As well as using it when a person has not brought anything to supervision, it can also be used at the beginning or end of a year to assist the person to get a snapshot of where they are at. Then it can be repeated with them at a different time, and used to compare answers, to reflect on different ways the person is answering the questions *over time*.

The 'Having a Voice Tool' is a great activity to use with people who have trouble *reflecting* as it really slows everything down and gets them to <u>stop,</u> <u>focus</u> and <u>reflect</u>.

I had another supervisee that I used this tool with. When I asked how the activity was for them, they said:

"I feel worse now as I can't do anything I want to do due to my circumstances which I have no control over."

What would you say to that?

My first response was to panic and go:

"Oh no! Now what do I do? It hasn't worked!

I have made the situation worse!! "

I quickly regrouped and said:

"What is it like to find yourself in this situation?"

The person shared what it was like and then...

HAD AN AHA MOMENT!

It was in these final moments of the supervision session that the realisation hit my supervisee:

They had clarity on what was really going on for them.

I could have easily sabotaged this moment of realisation by letting my perceived failure take me to a mental place where I made it *all about me* and whether or not I had *done a good job* or *chosen the right activity.*

You just never know what is about to happen...

As I often say to my supervision students:

"You just need to trust the process!!"

HAVING A VOICE TOOL

Step 1: Draw a picture of yourself

Step 2: Add something to your picture that makes it uniquely you

Step 3: Write answers to the following questions next to the parts of your body, as follows:

Mouth: *What do you want to say?*   *(One answer)*

Ears: *What do you want to hear?*   *(Two answers)*

Eyes: *What do you want to see?*   *(Two answers)*

Nose: *What do you want to smell?*   *(One answer)*

Brain: *What do you want to think about?*   *(One answer)*

Hands: *What do you want to do?*   *(Two answers)*

Feet: *Where do you want to go?*   *(Two answers)*

Heart: *What is in your heart?*   *(As many answers as you want)*

Arms: *Where do you get your strength?*   *(Two answers)*

Step 4: Reflect on the findings of this activity:

➭ "What do you notice now you have completed this activity?"

➭ "What has emerged for you?"

➭ "Have you noticed any themes?"

➭ "Does anything surprise you about what you have written?"

➭ "What does this mean for you now?"

A reflective tool I use when working in pastoral supervision is the 'Theological Reflection Model':

Theological Reflection

For those of you who are working as pastoral supervisors, you may find the model I created on theological reflection helpful. The model can also be used by anyone who finds it to be suitable to the context in which they are working or supporting others.

When I was engaging in chaplaincy training through Clinical Pastoral Education (CPE), theological reflection was an important aspect of reflecting on the interactions that we had with people.

My placements were in hospital settings and after visiting people in the wards, we came back and reflected on our experiences via group and individual supervision.

I undertook 3 x 400 hour CPE units and found it to be an incredibly rich, life-changing experience.

We mainly used *verbatims* to reflect on our encounters. A *verbatim* is where we would write, *word for word,* what happened. We would often role play our verbatims in the group supervision sessions.

It was amazing to see the difference it made to a conversation when we underwent the process of writing a verbatim then role playing the situation. We got to see the way we responded, by slowing it all down and really noticing what was happening for both the person and the person they were interacting with.

Once we had written a verbatim, we often added a spiritual assessment and a theological reflection to assist us to get an overall picture of what may have been going on the for the person and to get a sense of where God was in the encounter.

There were people from all different faiths and beliefs doing CPE so each person theologically reflected in a way that was meaningful for them.

For me, as a Christian, I found it wonderful to bring God into the reflection, as this was such a central part of my life.

The experience brought me even closer to God and I was able to reflect on the example of Jesus and the way that He interacted with people. This strengthened my personal relationship with Jesus.

I'm forever grateful for my CPE Supervisors for all that I learnt while engaging in my Chaplaincy training and also for introducing me to supervision. It was at this time that the seeds were planted for me to eventually become a supervisor myself.

Early on in my CPE training, I remember a time when I felt that I was 'trapped in a pit'. I had found myself in a situation where I just *couldn't see a way out.*

I took my situation to individual supervision, and we worked on this together using theological reflection. My supervisor said to me:

"It seems *now* as though you can't get out, that you are in an impossible situation but if you are prepared to *enter the process of supervision* then one day, you will be at the top of the pit and you will simply *step out.*"

I just couldn't see it, but I trusted my supervisor.

You may chuckle to yourself as you read what I said to her...

"Okay, tell me what I need to do, and I will **do it now**!!

Let's just get this done."

My supervisor had laughed respectfully...

"What?" I'd enquired, puzzled. "What did I say that was so funny?"

We had worked together for a while by this stage and had a great, safe relationship. She knew that I was an *action person* and would be impatient to <u>get started</u>.

Working on this situation with my supervisor was my first real understanding of entering the supervision process. I came to realise that 'stepping out of the pit' wasn't something that I could simply do 'there and then' just because:

⇨ I wanted to

⇨ I felt ready

⇨ I was brave enough to face it

In order to step out of the pit, I had to <u>do the work</u>!

*I had to **enter** the process of supervision!*

Step by step, I needed to build the scaffolding that would get me closer to the top!

As I worked with my supervisor, I was being transformed into the person that I needed to be to be <u>able</u> to step out of the pit. Or, as I reflect now, maybe I was 'filling in the pit' until it *wasn't as deep...*

Either way, eventually, I one day realised that I was at the top of the pit, and *I stepped out!!! What a day that was!*

I trusted the process and had found my way to freedom!

The Biblical story of Joseph was meaningful for me in my theological reflection and helped me along the way. What an amazing feeling it was to finally *feel free*, just as Joseph had in his story.

Maybe you feel like you are in a pit and can't get out. If so, can I encourage you to find a trained supervisor who is right for you and start the process. I'm sure, deep in my heart, you will not regret it!

I still use theological reflections a lot. It really helps me to consider where God is in a situation for myself.

I have developed a 'Theological Reflection Model' to use in supervision that I have used literally hundreds of times. I use it in pastoral supervision with people who I've contracted with who would like to look at what they bring to supervision through a theological lens, such as: pastors, ministers, chaplains, pastoral care workers, other people who work in these fields and anyone who wishes to reflect theologically.

Theological Reflection Model

Where is God for you?   **Where is God for them?**

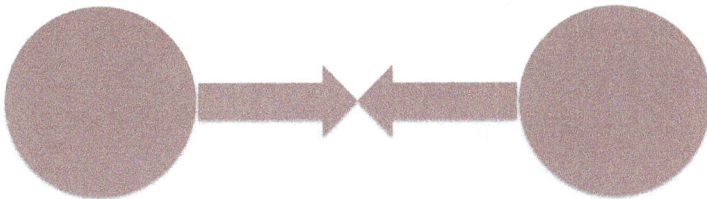

Where is God in between?
Sacred Moment

© Susan Marcuccio 2018

THEOLOGICAL REFLECTION MODEL

The Theological Reflection Model can be used at any time, on your own or when you are supporting someone. It is a great model to use in reflective practice, such as in a pastoral supervision session, particularly in the reflective space.

I use it differently each time, depending on the situation and on the person's beliefs. If the supervisee has expressed a particular faith and would like their spirituality included in the sessions, then this is a very powerful model to use.

When I use the model in supervision, I usually invite the supervisee to *draw* the whole model for themselves, on a piece of paper. This works for face to face and online sessions.

I ask them which side they would like to look at first:

➪ *"Where is God for You?"*

or

➪ *"Where is God for Them?"*

I then go on to ask the following questions, based on the order in which they have indicated they would like to proceed:

Where is God for you?

➪ What do you need?

➪ What is the cry of your heart?

➪ Where is God for you?

Where is God for them?

⇨ What do they need?

⇨ What is the cry of their heart?

⇨ Where is God for them?

Where is God in between?

⇨ Can you see the sacred moment?

Using the Theological Reflection Model

I remember a time when a chaplain came to supervision feeling very deflated about a chaplaincy encounter she had. She felt she had let the person down in the visit as the person was dying and she felt she just hadn't done enough to help them.

We decided to use the Theological Reflection Model to reflect on the situation. The chaplain chose to reflect first on the person they had visited, that is, to explore: Where is God for them?

I asked her to consider the first question, by saying:

"What do you think the person you visited needed on this day?"

She took some time to think about this and replied:

"Someone to be with her."

She had told me earlier that the person wasn't able to have family visit at this time and was very alone.

"Okay," I said. "Stay with this..."

The chaplain nodded. I then asked:

"What do you think was the cry of her heart on this day?"

She replied:

"She seemed so relieved when I came in to sit with her. I think the cry of her heart was to not be alone in her suffering."

There was some time of silence as we both digested this reality. I then said:

"Let's leave that there for a moment. Now let's focus on you."

With that, we began to explore: Where is God for You?

"On this day, what were *you* needing?"

She pondered on this for a while…

"I needed to feel like I was doing something, to make a difference, to be there for her. But I feel like I failed."

We stayed in that moment for a while as she allowed herself to express the depth of her feelings. I then asked her:

"What was the cry of *your heart* on this day?"

She answered:

"For her to know that I cared and that I was there for her and was there *with her*."

This was an incredibly moving moment as we both reflected on this.

After a time, I invited her to move now to consider where God was for her. I asked the question:

"If God was watching over her and saw what she was needing and heard the cry of her heart on this day to not be alone in her suffering, what might He have done?"

She replied:

"God would have thought: *Who can I send so she is not alone?*"

I then asked:

"And what about you? If God was watching over you, what would He have seen you were needing on this day and what the cry of your heart was?"

She answered:

"He would have seen that I desperately wanted to *make a difference* and to *be there* for this lady."

As we worked with this together, I invited her to write down in the model the questions and answers that we were pondering.

I then asked her to look at what she had written and where she felt God was for her and where God was for the other person.

She then suddenly said:

"God sent me to be with her!!!!"

The chaplain had an incredible moment of clarity, an aha moment:

"Oh, wow! God *sent me* to be with her, so she was not alone. He was there *for her* by sending someone to be with her in her moment of suffering!! And, God was there *for me* by allowing me to do something so meaningful - being with someone in their suffering, to really make a difference. I totally didn't see it, but now I do!!! Thank you, thank you!! Wow, God was really there *with us both.*"

This was such an incredible moment for the two of us in the session. We stayed there for a while and then I invited her to look again at the model. This time, I drew her attention to the centre of the model and we looked at the question: <u>Where is God in between?</u>

"When you think about the time that you had together, can you remember a moment during the visit when you felt that you had a *real connection* with her?"

What we are doing here is looking for the sacred moment, the moment that there was a connection and God was there with them both.

"Yes," the chaplain replied. "When she asked me to hold her hand and I sat with her - we didn't say anything. I didn't know what to say... I felt like such a failure. But now I can see...

That was actually the sacred moment!!!

It was good that I didn't say anything – wow!

The moment when I thought I was failing her *was actually* the sacred moment that she really wanted. This is blowing my mind...

I didn't see it then but now - *I see it so clearly*.

Thank you. Wow!"

I then suggested we do the final step in this activity.

"When you think of this encounter now with this lady, does it remind you of a Bible story, or a Bible character, or a scripture?"

She immediately said:

"It made me think of the Bible story when Jesus left the flock and went to find the one who was on their own. This is such a powerful image for me."

250

This final step had anchored the experience to her faith. I was careful not to add my own meanings during any part of this, I was simply asking the questions, allowing her to find and see for herself a sacred moment. It also showed her that she did indeed do what she had hoped to do:

*Show she cared and that she was there **for her** and there **with her**.*

The chaplain wanted to feel like she had made a difference, to feel like she had done something, and had been there *for her*. Looking through this theological lens, God had brought together someone who was alone and suffering with someone who wanted to be with someone and let them know they were not alone in their suffering.

It sounds like a sacred God moment to me...

You will find many other models, tools and resources throughout this book that can be used in reflective practice.

CHAPTER TEN

GROUP SUPERVISION

Be creative
Be free
Join a group
Listen to the other voices
Get connected
Belong

See things differently
Look again
Be a contributor
You have things to offer
Trust the process
Engage with the others

Be held
Be together
Try again
Get your aha moment
Be encouraged
Off you go

Group Supervision

While I love engaging with people in *individual* supervision, I have found incredible richness in working together with others *in group supervision*. There is something so encouraging to know that others have similar struggles and challenges when working with people.

As supervisors, mentors, chaplains and others in the helping professions, we often work in isolation and can wonder what other people are doing in their practice. We may even wonder whether we are 'hitting the mark'.

I have found that when people engage in group supervision which is such an encouraging space, they leave the session feeling invigorated and validated. They learn *not just from* what they bring but *from hearing others present* and seeing how *the group* assists the person to see the situation from a new or different perspective to gain greater clarity.

Group supervision provides a safe, confidential space for those in the helping professions to join with others to reflect on their work practices and experiences, and to gain a better understanding of the impact of these experiences. As we know, supervision is a vital part of maintaining health and wellbeing: engaging in *group supervision* is another way to access this type of support for your professional role. It helps you to understand yourself better and to reflect on your responses to situations.

The benefits of having group supervision include receiving support from the group, having a non-judgmental place for accountability, a place to debrief with others, and the provision of a rich learning environment.

In group supervision, each person brings specific cases or situations to discuss and reflect on with the group. The group supervisor ensures that the process of supervision occurs and facilitates the session.

I usually run group supervision with a minimum of four and a maximum of eight participants. These groups are either face to face or online. The groups run for two hours with four people bringing something to present for half an hour each.

After running face to face group supervision for many years, I never dreamed that engaging with a group *online* would be such a wonderful and meaningful experience. It is now the main way that I provide group supervision. It is much more accessible for people and many of the groups I run have people from all over Australia taking part.

Groups can be made up of all supervisors and mentors. They bring aspects of a supervision or mentoring session they would like to get some understanding of, such as what was going on for them in the session and/or for the person they were supervising or mentoring at the time. They may have come away from a session with questions about whether they really connected with their supervisee/mentee or if they provided the session that the supervisee/mentee was after.

No matter what reason they have for coming to group supervision, supervisors and mentors are able to attend knowing they are in a safe supportive space where they can reflect and ponder questions about their practice. The group supervisor manages the environment at all times by facilitating effective and meaningful interactions whilst ensuring that there is no mention of any details that might enable an individual or organisation to be identified.

Others who might benefit from group supervision could include anyone in a helping profession or any other type of profession who wants to reflect on their practice, their work or their interactions in a group setting.

In my experience, having a trained facilitator is essential as managing the group dynamics is harder than it looks, and you need someone who knows how to 'hold the group', keep it safe and stay very focused on the task at hand. The group facilitator also needs to be able to read the room and to get a sense of what's happening for the *group as a whole* as well as how *each individual* is experiencing the session.

Preparing for Group Supervision

As a group facilitator, I send out an information sheet which includes the following questions. I do this ahead of time (prior to when the group first meets) so they can use the questions when it's their turn to present:

1. Briefly describe the case/situation that you are bringing to group supervision
2. Explain the particular aspect of the case/situation that you'd like to explore
3. Discuss why you have brought this particular case/situation
4. Tell the group what you would like to get from the group by bringing this today

I encourage participants to prepare before the session so that they can read their case or situation out to the group when it is their turn. They don't need to distribute copies of their notes before or during the session, the preparation is really to help *them* to get focused and clear about what they would like to bring and what they would like to get from the session.

I also ask participants to maintain confidentiality by not disclosing the actual name of a person or organisation.

If a participant has not written down the material that they want to present, I facilitate their presentation by asking them each of the questions as the session unfolds. I find this system works well and assists me to keep the participant focused and clear with their material.

I have found it's really important that the group *enters* the process of supervision as this assists the person presenting to see the situation from new perspectives. For group supervision, you can use a process model such as the 'Perspective Supervision Process Model' found in Chapter Four or you can try the 'New Perspectives Creative Group Supervision Model' outlined later in this chapter.

The process starts with the presenter describing the case or situation that they're bringing. While the experience the person brings is to be held with respect, the group doesn't need to know all the details. If the group gets *too caught up in the details of the case or situation*, then the process never gets going.

Let's look at how the process of supervision unfolds when there are multiple participants. We find ourselves, as a group, with a situation or issue that the person has brought in, and we all figuratively *walk around it* and *look at it* from a different or new perspective. This act of reflection slows down our collective thinking and we often see things we've not seen before.

Imagine how amazing the supervision process is when we do it as a group! It often becomes such a sacred space...

The person who brought the situation or issue is supported by the group while they make meaning out of what could have originally seemed such an unclear position to be in. Multiple perspectives from different group members provide the opportunity for a broader view of the situation.

Every time I engage with a group for group supervision, I learn something and am deeply moved by having the opportunity and privilege to be part of such a connected group. I find that the people who come to group supervision put such a high value on growing as a person both personally and professionally.

The types of things that people bring to group supervision are:

⇨ Case studies

⇨ How to work with a particular individual or group

⇨ Work conflict or challenges

⇨ Looking for clarity or new perspectives around a situation

⇨ A supervision, mentoring or chaplaincy encounter

⇨ Other scenarios (usually centred around the person's work)

Creative Group Supervision

After having such great success using *creative tools* online with *individual* supervision, I decided to try using *creative tools* as part of the process of *group* supervision.

Unsure of how this might go, I advertised places for three Creative Group Supervision groups which would meet throughout the year. All three groups filled up quickly. I saw this as an indication that people were looking for different ways to experience supervision and to connect with others in a real and authentic way.

Once I started delivering the online sessions, I was excited to learn about the reasons people had registered for creative group supervision. In addition to wanting to engage in the process of group supervision, it seemed that many participants were wanting to learn about creative tools so they could use them in the individual or group supervision sessions that they were providing.

The first day of the first session, I had an idea of how using creative tools with a group might go but it was something new. So, while I was confident that I could incorporate creative tools into a group setting whilst trusting the process of supervision, I held some apprehension.

I invited each person in the group to introduce themselves and to also name a colour that would give the group some insight into who they were. It was incredible to see how something as simple and creative as *introducing yourself as a colour* could bond the group and start us on our journey together of creative group supervision.

I shared that my colour to describe myself on that day was red, as it represented for me the passion I had towards supervision. I said that I wanted to have a voice and to be seen so I could be an advocate for others.

To me, red speaks of vibrancy and life, of having a go, being bold, making a mark. I really enjoyed this activity as it helped me to articulate things about myself that I wouldn't have shared if we had just introduced ourselves in a more traditional way.

I wonder if I asked you to describe yourself as a colour right now, what colour you would choose and what it would represent for you...

After we had discussed and decided together on the group guidelines such as confidentially, showing respect, being encouraging and supportive to each other and giving each person the opportunity to contribute, we began.

I had asked three people to bring something for the group to work with. The first person shared what they were bringing, why they chose this particular issue to bring to the group and what they were hoping to get from the group by bringing it.

I also asked the question: "By the time we have finished today, what do you hope to walk away with?"

This was to help the individual and the group to be very clear about what we were doing and what the focus was.

Once the person had shared all this, I considered which creative tool we could use as a group to reflect on what they had brought.

I had not asked the participants to bring anything creative with them to the session. I did this on purpose as my goal was to model how we could work creatively *without preparation*, by working with what was in the room. In this case, as we were online, we were actually working with what was in each participant's room.

I decided with this first case to invite the person presenting to choose some objects in their room to represent the different people in the story. I also asked the other people in the group to choose *just one object* that represented the situation they had just heard.

I asked the presenter to put the items in front of them and to share with the group:

➡ what objects they had chosen to represent each person

➡ what had drawn them to choose each object

➡ what they noticed about the objects

➡ what they noticed as they looked at them all together

As a group supervisor, as with individual supervision, it is important not to analyse what a participant chooses or to put your own meaning onto it. Let them share what they see and what it means for them.

A simple activity such as choosing objects from the room helps the person to get into a different headspace and see the situation in a different way. I'm constantly amazed at how using creative tools seems to unlock something. People get such clarity and see their situation from a new perspective.

It can be the object itself that reveals something or the different sizes of the objects they choose. Sometimes, it's where they have placed the objects in relation to each other. Other times, people don't choose an object for one of the people in the situation which can *also* tell them something.

Even just going through the process of selecting and talking about the objects can be enough for the person to get the insight they were after.

I then usually open it up to the group to ask any questions for clarification, to offer something they have noticed or to give a word of encouragement. We need to make sure that it doesn't become an interrogation, and that the group is respectful of the situation and again, doesn't put their *own* meaning on what the person has brought or chosen.

It's not a time for the group to be sharing their *own* story, even if they think it relates. However, group participants can, at this point, ask to share about the object *they chose* and offer any relevant insight they may have. In doing so, these individual contributions might also help the person who has brought the situation to gain new perspectives.

I love seeing creative tools being used this way by the wider group – it seems to really broaden the understanding of the experience for the person presenting the situation and group members also benefit through seeing the learning process unfold.

As the group facilitator, it's important to ensure that the group interactions are managed well. If the group starts to put too much focus *on the presenter* rather than on what has been brought to group supervision, I might step in to remind the group of the guidelines we all agreed on.

There may be aspects of what the presenter has brought to group supervision that may be more appropriate for individual supervision due to its sensitive nature. If this happens, I stop the group and indicate that we won't continue with this aspect of the subject and invite the presenter to consider taking it to individual supervision with their own supervisor. The role of group facilitator is to ensure the group and each individual feels safe while they're in the group and to maintain an encouraging and supportive environment.

Once the group has had the opportunity to contribute, I usually check in with the presenter and ask them what is emerging for them from doing the reflective activity with the creative tool. I also make sure that we are keeping with the focus that they have chosen for this session and we're not getting off track.

It's incredible what does emerge from these sessions. Using creative tools is a wonderful way to reflect.

At the end of the presentation, I ask for any final words from the group. I find that group members often provide words of encouragement at this point which is another positive aspect of conducting supervision in a group setting.

I then ask the presenter what they are taking away from the presentation in regards to the focus area. It's so interesting to hear about the new perspectives they have gained and also, what this clarity means for them and what action they make take as a result. Other group members might also reflect on what they have learned by having the privilege of being present.

Group supervision often leads the presenter to engage in further reflection which they may undertake after the session either on their own or with someone else they trust such as their individual supervisor.

With other creative group supervision sessions, I've used a range of different creative tools, for example: the 'Draw Your Situation Tool'. When I adapt this tool to use in a group setting, I invite the presenter to be the person who draws the situation (as per the method described in chapter nine). I also invite the other participants in the group to draw the situation *as they have heard it* and find that this brings powerful results.

The presenter shares with the group what they have noticed about the picture they have drawn and follows through the steps outlined in the tool.

Once we have completed the drawing aspect of the exercise, I open it up to the group and invite them to ask questions or to offer something. This could also be the time the others in the room show the picture that they have drawn. This can offer a wonderfully different perspective of the situation which can be very helpful for the presenter.

It is imperative that the facilitator and the rest of the group don't offer advice or try to fix the situation. It's also important not to try and interpret what the presenter has brought: the idea is to slow down and trust the process of supervision - or in this case, the process of group supervision!

I really want to stress that you need to be trained to run group supervision as it can quickly 'derail' if you are not careful. Managing the dynamics of the group, staying on track and not going off on tangents are all challenges you can face when facilitating a group.

When I run 'Group Supervision Training' to train group facilitators, I engage the group in a typical group supervision session. The difference is, when I'm training facilitators, I'm very overt about the process and may even suddenly stop the session to talk about what's happening in the group.

After each person has presented, we stop and reflect on what they are noticing about *what I am doing* as the facilitator, so the learning is very experiential. I gradually give people the opportunity to have a turn at being the facilitator and I co-facilitate with them. Then, as a group, we reflect on what we were both doing as facilitators and this provides valuable feedback for the person on their developing facilitator skills.

If you are interested in becoming a group supervisor, my suggestion would be to follow these steps:

⇨ Engage in group supervision as a participant

⇨ Train and work as a supervisor

⇨ Undertake training in facilitating group supervision

As you can see from these steps, there's quite a bit involved in becoming a group supervisor. If you think this sounds like you, the rewards of facilitating group supervision can be great!

Planning to Run Creative Group Supervision

I find that there are a number of important things to consider when planning to run creative group supervision (as opposed to using creative tools in individual supervision).

To help capture my thoughts and experiences with creative group supervision so far, I developed the 'New Perspectives Creative Group Supervision Model'.

I made this new model (which I will refer to as the *group model*) as I felt creative group supervision needed its own road map, rather than simply 'running a group' using the road map from the 'Perspective Supervision Process Model' (the *process model*).

NEW PERSPECTIVES CREATIVE GROUP SUPERVISION MODEL

As we look at the *group model* below, we can see that some of the elements are the same or similar to the *process model*, however, some elements are brand new:

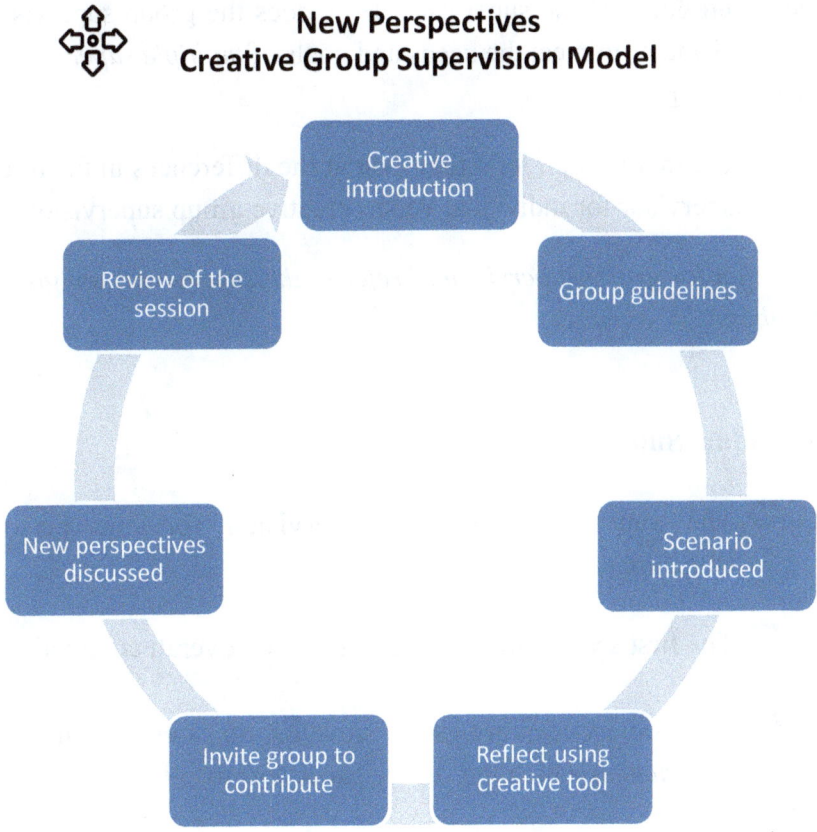

New Perspectives Creative Group Supervision Model

- Creative introduction
- Group guidelines
- Scenario introduced
- Reflect using creative tool
- Invite group to contribute
- New perspectives discussed
- Review of the session

© Susan Marcuccio 2022

Different Road Maps

The aim of Creative Group Supervision is for the group members to *enter* the process of supervision. The road map, as shown in the group model, follows a similar path to the process model road map, however, as we look more closely, we can see there are *differences.*

265

One explanation for the different road maps is the change in the demands on the supervisor (referred to as the group facilitator) in group supervision.

We know from earlier reading that the supervisor 'leads and adapts' the supervision session *in the moment*, according to the expressed needs and goals of the supervisee. How does the group supervisor 'lead and adapt' to meet the needs and goals of *multiple supervisees*, all at the same time?

To explore this further, let's first look at the differences in the roles of the supervisor for individual versus creative group supervision.

Note that for group supervision, I refer to the supervisees as 'group members'.

Individual Supervision:

➪ The supervisor provides supervision for one person (the *supervisee*)

➪ The first session includes setting of the 'overall contract'

➪ The supervisee brings a situation to supervision (the *experience*) which the supervisor *listens* to

➪ The supervisor and supervisee enter the process of supervision together to look more closely at the supervisee's situation (progressing through the elements of *contract, focus, reflection, summary, action* and *review*)

➪ The session ends with the supervisee having greater clarity around the situation they brought

Creative Group Supervision:

➡ The group supervisor provides supervision for the *group members*

➡ The group supervisor facilitates the session, starting with a *creative introduction* and establishing *group guidelines*

➡ One at a time, a group member brings a situation to share (*introduces a scenario)* and the group listens

➡ The group enters the process of supervision together (facilitated by the group supervisor)

➡ The process of supervision is centred around assisting the presenter to *reflect using a creative tool* on the situation they have brought to supervision

➡ The session ends with the presenter having greater clarity around the situation they brought

➡ The group supervisor facilitates the involvement of the group members in the supervision process by carefully involving them in the element of *reflect using creative tool* whilst making sure that the interactions stay with the focus that the presenter has chosen for the session and that the group does not get off track.

The Elements in the Group Model

This group model is drawn as a circle in a similar way to the process model. Each element represents the steps taken by the group as they work their way collectively through the 'flow' of the supervision process, under the guidance of the group facilitator (the supervisor).

The elements that I have included in the group model are:

⇨ Creative introduction

⇨ Group guidelines

⇨ Scenario introduced

⇨ Reflect using creative tool

⇨ Invite group to contribute

⇨ New perspectives discussed

⇨ Review of the session

Meeting for the First Time

Group members are not typically the supervisees of the group supervisor. Therefore, on the day of the first group supervision session, the group members and the group supervisor will all likely be meeting *for the first time*.

To assist the group to meet and settle into the session, I have included the element: *Creative Introduction* in the group model.

For the creative introduction, I like to use an activity like the one mentioned earlier (introducing oneself as a colour). There are other ways that the introductions could be undertaken.

Group Guidelines

It's important to allow the group to form and all take ownership of the group process. Allow the group to discuss and decide together on the group guidelines. I prefer this language rather than group rules.

Some of the guidelines I suggest you include are:

➡ Confidentiality
(Unless there is a duty of care or mandatory reporting situation disclosed)

➡ Respect

➡ Allowing all participants to have a voice

➡ No giving of advice

➡ No saying how a person could have done it better

➡ No sharing of your own stories when it takes away from the presenter's story

➡ Be encouraging

➡ Keep to time

Keeping to time is so important in group supervision. Therefore, I'd like to point out the following before moving onto the introducing the scenario.

For creative group supervision, I usually have sessions that go for two hours and three people present for thirty minutes each:

➡ In the first group session, the other thirty minutes is used to do the introductions and establish the group guidelines

➡ In subsequent sessions, the other thirty minutes is taken up discussing the creative tools we have used in the session (ten minutes between each presentation)

In group supervision, it's important to be very deliberate about the relationship we have as group members. So only fairly major things are shared otherwise we just go straight to the first person presenting. This helps keep the boundary in the group supervisory relationships.

The only exception to this is if something significant has occurred that is relevant to mention at the start. I therefore usually ask at the beginning of each session:

"Is there anything anyone needs to share with the group before we start?"

For example, when I asked this question at the start of a session, one person advised that a close family member had died only a few weeks earlier.

Another person shared that they were in temporary accommodation after not being able to be in their home and they had limited internet.

Both of these situations were appropriate to be shared as they helped the other group members to be mindful during the session.

Beginning, Middle and End of Presentation

A strategy for ensuring that all elements are included in each thirty minute presentation is to divide the time into three sections: beginning, middle and end.

- ⇨ Beginning (*scenario introduced*),
- ⇨ Middle (*reflect using creative tool* and *group contribution*)
- ⇨ End (*new perspectives discussed* and *review of the session*)

Make sure you have a clock handy so you can monitor the time. For example, if the person is taking too long introducing the scenario, respectfully intervene to assist them to move to the next element in a timely manner.

While the story they are sharing is very important, we don't actually need to know all the details. If you stay too long on the story, you may run out of time to enter the process of supervision.

In your language throughout the session, be clearly communicating to the group what's happening at each point, such as:

"We are *now* going to do this or that…"

As you are getting nearer to the end of the thirty minute presentation time, you might find it helpful to use the following sentence starters:

⇨ "As we start to get close to finishing today…"

⇨ "In the five minutes we have left…"

⇨ "As we finish up this presentation…"

This way, people know we are coming to the end of the presentation. Then make sure *you finish right on time*.

You may like to take a short break for a few minutes in between presentations, especially if you're doing it online. However, if you do take short breaks, remember to adjust your timing so you still finish on time.

In summary, timing is so important as if you are still in reflection mode at the end of a presentation, the person will not have the opportunity to complete the end part of the process, and you risk leaving them in a vulnerable place.

So, keep tracking the whole way through to ensure you have sufficient time for the beginning, middle and end sections of each presentation.

GROUP MODEL IN ACTION

Let's look at the other elements of the group model (and how they relate to the process model). Then, let's see the group model in action as we go through the example of using the creative tool of *metaphors*:

⇨ *Scenario introduced* is where we cover an abridged version of the supervision elements from the process model (*experience, listen, contract* and *focus*)

⇨ *Reflect using a creative tool* and *invite group to contribute* relate to the element of *reflect* from the process model

⇨ *New perspectives discussed* and *review of the session* relate to the process model elements of *summary, action* and *review*

Using Metaphors in Creative Group Supervision

One of the creative tools I use in group supervision is to use metaphors. I ask the person presenting to think of a metaphor or image that comes to mind when they think about the situation they are bringing to supervision.

Another way is to listen out for any metaphors or images that might come up when the person is describing the situation.

Let's look at an example of a metaphor being used in a group supervision session:

The presenter might be talking about a situation they have brought to supervision with a focus on the relationship with someone they are working with. At this point, I have not mentioned using metaphors as a creative tool however, as they are sharing about the situation, I hear them say:

"I feel like I'm 'walking on eggshells' whenever I'm with this person."

I could then suggest we use metaphors as the creative tool for this presentation. I then may say:

"I heard you mention the feeling of 'walking on eggshells'. I wonder if you could stay with that metaphor for a moment and tell us some more about that."

I then might ask:

"What's it like to walk on eggshells?"

The person might reply by saying something like:

"It's uncomfortable. I'm worried about taking the next step. Eggshells can easily break, so I feel like I have to go gently and carefully all the time, which is exhausting."

I would invite the presenter to continue on and share anything else they have noticed about the metaphor: what it may mean for them in relation to the *situation they are reflecting on* and specifically, what it may mean regarding what they were *hoping to get from the session.*

As I've mentioned before, it's really important not to analyse or put your own meaning onto the metaphor. However, as the facilitator, you may offer a new perspective or share something you noticed that the presenter may not have seen.

I do sometimes ask the person to consider a *different metaphor* for how they would like the situation to be, and we then tease this metaphor out in a similar way. They can then compare the two metaphors and consider what would need to happen for their situation to feel different in some way, so that being with the person at their work felt more like the *second metaphor.*

Your decisions and moves as the facilitator really depend on what's happening in the session - you have to practice 'being in the moment' and deciding 'as you go' what might be the most meaningful way to use any metaphors that come up.

'Thinking on your feet' like this takes some courage to do, but the results can be mind-blowing! The incredible revelation and aha moments people have in group supervision using these metaphors and images is truly amazing.

When I'm using metaphors in creative group supervision, I work in a number of different ways to include the members of the group in the supervision process. Again, it depends on the way I feel led to go in that session. I may ask the group to write down any *other* metaphors they heard the person say as they were sharing about their situation. Then, if and when appropriate, I would ask individuals in the group to share the metaphor or image they noticed with the presenter.

If the presenter hadn't specifically shared a metaphor, I may ask the group to think of a metaphor that comes to mind as they consider the story that the presenter has just offered. I would then invite individual members of the group to share that metaphor or image. This really adds to the experience for the presenter as they are offered a number of metaphors leading to a number of different perspectives. This *group sharing* of mental imagery can often help them to see things with greater clarity.

If the group have picked up on any other metaphors that have come up when the presenter was describing the situation, then it may be appropriate for them to also share these with the presenter, to add to the overall picture. If the presenter writes down the metaphors as the group members share, they can take these ideas with them in order to continue the reflection after the session.

There are many other considerations in group supervision that are similar to individual supervision but are often amplified when in a group such as being aware of transference, countertransference and parallel processing, noticing themes, entering the emotional zone and being aware of emotional boundaries. You will find reference to these in other chapters.

In summary, working in a group is another way to gain new perspectives in supervision, to feel supported, gain insight and engage in transformational learning!

Conclusion

Now that you have come to the end of this book, my hope is that you have been inspired and encouraged. That you have been thinking about your own unique calling, being able to 'connect in' with what you are passionate about, and that if you haven't already found it, you are *closer* to finding your purpose and that which gives you life. That you have found your lane and can stay in it.

By sharing some of my story, you may now understand what underpins the concepts that I have introduced in this book, and you got a sense of the motivation I have to do this meaningful work. Whether supervision is new for you or it's something you are very familiar with, I hope that you were able to gain clarity on this important subject and feel more equipped or have more understanding.

Being able to listen well is a skill and also requires us to be intentional about it. I hope that I highlighted well the importance of listening, providing support and showing those we come across that they are valued and that their story matters. Perhaps you have benefited from some of the lessons I learnt through hearing about some of the incredible people I have met along the way. I feel gratitude that I was able to share these stories with you and honour these people.

I wonder if you felt like you were able to unwrap the gift of supervision. If you are new to supervision, I hope you were excited to open this gift. If for a moment you saw it from my perspective, you would have seen why I'm so passionate about it. If supervision is not new to you then I hope that you gained a few gems along the way that have assisted you or perhaps it ignited or reignited the passion you have for supervision.

How amazing is the process of supervision? I was just blown away when I realised just how incredible it is and how we really can trust the process. While of course we need to always honour a person's story, sometimes we are more helpful to a person by assisting them to step out of their story and to gain new perspectives. Spending time going into detail of each step of the process using the model really helped me and I hope it has assisted you as well.

We touched on knowing how to navigate life and being resilient and were reminded that there are things that we can all do in preparation for what comes along. Some situations are so painful that nothing can ever really prepare you, but I am convinced that there are things we can do, and we covered some of these in this book. We need to get educated and know ourselves, to process our emotions as they come along and not let them build up. To understand that it's the internal things that can take us out not the external circumstances. That if we are connected to our calling this can give us the energy we need to keep going and to bounce forward.

We talked about how important the relationship is in supervision and that even if we technically follow the process but neglect to make a connection, we have missed the whole point. The privilege of walking alongside someone was highlighted, a powerful image to ponder. To be authentic and really care for someone, being aware of what's happening, to carefully consider our response and to always look to empower. To care and be cared for and to engage in ways that will enhance your work and life.

When I had the revelation that not everyone sees and experiences the world the same as me, it was life changing and really impacted the way that I interacted with people. As we explore this in this book, you may have also had a deeper understanding of this and how it gives us much more insight into what may be happening for a person. To ensure that we consider situations from the other person's perspective. If you looked at the vision and values exercise you may now have more clarity around whether you are more vision or values driven. The importance of continued personal and professional development was also covered.

Exploring emotions and boundaries in more depth and slowing down the whole process of an interaction with someone can assist us to make meaningful connections with others. As we looked at advanced empathy, validation, triggers, transference and reflecting feelings my hope is it has given you more insight and practical ways of being with someone and being able to communicate in a more mindful and deliberate way. Knowing more about and keeping appropriate boundaries in place was another area that I hope was helpful.

We delved into the topic of reflective practice and discussed how it is a such a foundational aspect of supervision. I was able to share some of the creative tools and resources that I have found helpful and offered you ways to consider reflecting for yourself and with those you journey with. As you engage in reflective practice it broadens your perspective and incredible things can happen. You may have now been inspired to be innovative yourself and create your own reflective tools.

You will have picked up in the chapter on group supervision, that I really enjoy this type of supervision and see it as a wonderful way to work together with others to be encouraged and to have our thinking stretched. You may now be considering starting or joining a group if you haven't already and I would encourage you to give it a go. Join a group or train to be able to facilitate a group or spice up your own group by introducing creative tools.

As I often say in supervision, now that we have finished this time together:

> *"What do you feel you are taking with you:*
> *in this case from this book?"*

You may like to spend some time reflecting on the highlights for you and what any new insights you have gained might mean for you now.

What action steps will you now take after reading this book?

I see it as a real privilege that you have taken the time to journey with me. Thank you!

My hope is that you have gained many new perspectives and can live your life with greater clarity.

List of Models, Tools and Resources

MODELS

TOOLS

RESOURCES

Bibliography and Further Reading

Broughton, G. (2021). *A Practical Christology for Pastoral Supervision*. Routledge.

Carroll, M., & Gilbert, M. C. (2011). *On being a supervisee: Creating learning partnerships*. PsychOz Publications.

Carroll, M. (2014). *Effective supervision for the helping professions*. Sage.

Davys, A., & Beddoe, L. (2020). *Best practice in professional supervision: A guide for the helping professions*. Jessica Kingsley Publishers.

DeLong, W. R. (Ed.). (2009). *Courageous conversations: The teaching and learning of pastoral supervision*. University Press of America.

Frankl, V. E. (1985). *Man's search for meaning*. Simon and Schuster.

Hawkins, P., & McMahon, A. (2020). Supervision in the Helping Professions 5e.

Henderson, P., Millar, A., & Holloway, J. (2014). *Practical supervision: How to become a supervisor for the helping professions* (Vol. 20140421). Jessica Kingsley Publishers.

Hewson, D., & Carroll, M. (2016). Reflective supervision toolkit. *Hazelbrook, NSW: MoshPit*.

Hewson, D., & Carroll, M. (2016). *Reflective practice in supervision: companion volume to the reflective supervision toolkit*. Moshpit Publishing.

Hubbard, G., Rice, J., & Galvin, P. (2015). *Strategic management: thinking, analysis, action*. Pearson Australia.

Hunter, C. (2010). A reflection upon theological reflection. *Retrieved from Stirling*.

Katz, R. S., & Johnson, T. A. (Eds.). (2016). *When professionals weep: Emotional and countertransference responses in palliative and end-of-life care*. Routledge.

Leach, J., & Paterson, M. (2015). *Pastoral supervision: a handbook*. SCM Press.

Mezirow, J. (1997). Transformative learning: Theory to practice. *New directions for adult and continuing education, 1997*(74), 5-12.

Palmer, P. J. (2018). *On the brink of everything: Grace, gravity, and getting old*. Berrett-Koehler Publishers.

Paver, J. E. (2016). *Theological reflection and education for ministry: The search for integration in theology*. Routledge.

Paterson, M., & Rose, J. (Eds.). (2014). *Enriching ministry: Pastoral supervision in practice*. Canterbury Press.

Paterson, M. (2020). Between a Rock and a Hard Place: Pastoral Supervision Revisited and Revisioned.

Paterson, M., & Crumlish, L. (2021). Creative Approaches in Pastoral Supervision, IPSRP Publications.

Robinson, S. G., Hart, A., & Anderson, R. S. (2007). *Ministry in Disaster Settings: Lessons from the edge*. Stephen Robinson.

Rothschild, B. (2006). *Help for the helper: The psychophysiology of compassion fatigue and vicarious trauma*. WW Norton & Company.

Rothschild, B. (2010). *8 Keys to Safe Trauma Recovery: Take-Charge Strategies to Empower Your Healing (8 Keys to Mental Health)*. WW Norton & Company.

Shohet, R. (2011). *Supervision as transformation: A passion for learning*. Jessica Kingsley Publishers.

Steere, D. A. (2002). *The supervision of pastoral care*. Wipf and Stock Publishers.

Stroebe, M., & Schut, H. (2010). The dual process model of coping with bereavement: A decade on. *OMEGA-Journal of Death and Dying, 61*(4), 273-289.

Wosket, V., & Page, S. (2001). The cyclical model of supervision. *Integrative approaches to supervision, 30*, 13.

About the Author

Susan Marcuccio is the founder of **Perspective Supervision**, a supervision practice providing supervision and mentoring to supervisors, mentors, chaplains, pastors, leaders, pastoral care workers, business leaders and allied health professionals.

Susan trained as a Professional Pastoral Supervisor with Transforming Practices and has a Graduate Certificate in Professional Supervision (Clinical) (Pastoral) from St Marks Theological Centre. Her education includes a Diploma of Vocational Education and Training, and a Diploma of Training, Design and Development. She also holds a Graduate Certificate in Christian Leadership and a Master of Arts with a specialisation in Pastoral Ministry and Pastoral Supervision from Alphacrucis University College. Susan is a Recognised Supervisor, Mentor, Chaplain, Trainer and Assessor.

To access Susan's supervision and mentoring services, to book Susan as a conference or workshop presenter, or to purchase a range of supervision, mentoring and chaplaincy resources, visit:

www.perspectivesupervision.com.au

Susan is an Ordained Minister with Australia Christian Churches (ACC) and is part of the ACC NSW State Pastors Health Team and a member of Australian Christian Mentoring Network (ACMN).

Susan is a member of the **Australasian Association of Supervision** (AAOS) as a Supervisor Trainer as well as serving on the AAOS Board for over ten years.

Susan has been in various roles in AAOS, including the Chair of Training Standards which oversees the Membership Committee ensuring applicants meet the industry training standards required for Supervisor Trainers, Supervisors and Associates.

The Australasian Association of Supervision (AAOS) provides membership for supervisors, from clinical and pastoral contexts, as well as from other emerging fields that are seeing the value of supervision. Supervision professional development is provided as part of membership.

To find a Supervisor or a Recognised Supervisor Training Program (RSTP) or to apply for membership, visit:

www.supervision.org.au

Susan is the National Supervision Director for **Chaplaincy Australia** (CA), having establishing the CA National Supervision and Mentoring Program which recognises the training and experience of Professional Pastoral Supervisors and Mentors.

Susan works with a dedicated National Leadership Team of supervisors and mentors providing 'Connection and Content' gatherings for members, regular 'Professional Development' and 'Supervision GAP Training' for members and non-members.

Susan was the initiator of the inaugural CA National Supervision and Mentoring Conference 'Innovation' connecting supervisors, mentors and chaplains from all over Australia. Susan and her team also provide and facilitate Group Supervision, including Creative Group Supervision and Group Supervision Training.

Susan is passionate about supporting and equipping trainee supervisors and mentors and has also established an intern program for those who have completed their supervision training and are working towards gaining enough practice hours to become a Recognised Supervisor.

To find a Professional Supervisor, Supervision Intern or Mentor, to apply for membership or to access one of the many programs and services available, visit:

www.chaplaincyaustralia.com/supervision

Susan previously held roles with ***Chaplaincy Australia*** including: National Training Director and NSW/ACT State Director. She has been in various other chaplaincy roles including hospital, emergency services and disaster response chaplaincy.

Susan has a Certificate IV in Christian Chaplaincy & Pastoral Care and completed 3 x 400 hr Clinical Pastoral Education (CPE) units.

Susan served on the CPE Council for the NSW College of CPE and the Civil Chaplaincies Advisory Committee. Susan was also part of a Subject Matter Expert Group (SMEG) assisting with the development of nationally recognised chaplaincy training.

To find out more about chaplaincy, visit:

www.chaplaincyaustralia.com

NOTES